Beating Around the Bush

Beating Around the Bush

ART BUCHWALD

Introduction by Garry Trudeau

Mike Luckovich

Seven Stories Press

NEW YORK - LONDON - MELBOURNE - TORONTO

First trade paperback edition, September 2006

Seven Stories Press
140 Watts Street
New York, NY 10013
http://www.sevenstories.com/

In Canada
Publishers Group Canada, 250A Carlton Street, Toronto, ON M5A 2L1

In the UK
Turnaround Publisher Services Ltd., Unit 3, Olympia Trading Estate, Coburg Road, Wood Green, London N22 6TZ

In Australia
Palgrave Macmillan, 627 Chapel Street, South Yarra, VIC 3141

College professors may order examination copies of Seven Stories Press titles for a free six-month trial period. To order, visit www.sevenstories.com/textbook/ or send a fax on school letterhead to 212.226.1411.

Book design by Jon Gilbert

Library of Congress Cataloging-in-Publication Data
Buchwald, Art.
  Beating around the bush / Art Buchwald.—1st ed.
    p. cm.
  ISBN-13: 978-1-58322-714-5 (hardcover: alk. paper) / ISBN-10: 1-58322-714-8 (hardcover: alk. paper)
  ISBN-13: 978-1-58322-750-3 (paperback: alk. paper) / ISBN-10: 1-58322-750-4 (paperback: alk. paper)
  1. United States—Politics and government—2001—Humor. I. Title.
PS3503.U1828B43 2005
814'.54—dc22

                                                    2005012063

Printed in Canada

9 8 7 6 5 4 3 2 1

EVERY WRITER WHO CAN'T SPELL or is never grammatically correct needs an editor. Cathy Crary has fit this role since 1982. I therefore dedicate this book to her. She laughs at everything, but still wields a red pencil in her left hand.

CONTENTS

············

Preface to the Paperback Edition

WHEN *BEATING AROUND THE BUSH* was published in hardcover I had two legs and great kidneys. Now I have one leg and wounded kidneys. The paperback version of *Beating Around the Bush* had nothing to do with these losses.

Bush is still captain of the *Titanic*. There are icebergs all over Washington. Some of the White House stars have left the ship. Some of them have become lobbyists, some have escaped indictment, and others have been writing books.

Despite all this, nothing has changed since the hardcover, except that several columns have been added and the beating has not stopped.

The main difference is that the softcover is much cheaper.

The good thing is, although I went to a hospice, I haven't died. It has made my publisher very happy.

Preface to the First Edition

BEFORE I BEGIN, I would like to say that I am prepared to go to jail rather than reveal to a grand jury the names of my sources for this book. The reason is I had no sources—I made everything up.

The characters I mention, such as President George W. Bush, Donald Rumsfeld, Condoleezza Rice, former Attorney General John Ashcroft, Bill O'Reilly, Arnold Schwarzenegger, Martha Stewart, Michael Jackson, Vladimir Putin, Saddam Hussein, Osama bin Laden, Jacques Chirac, Tony Blair, Prince Charles, and the Boston Red Sox, are all fictitious and do not resemble anyone living, dead, or in between.

It is hard to believe, but for all of us these have been the best of times and the worst of times—depending on if you are in the top two percent of wealthiest Americans, have health insurance, a decent pension plan, and a credit card that doesn't bounce on you.

These past few years have been a gold mine of material for a columnist. For one reason, our leaders keep screwing up and refuse to admit it. As you will read, there are no bad guys in Washington, there are only good guys doing bad things.

The uppermost subject on our minds has been single-sex marriage. No civilized society can have people of the same gender getting into bed together. Then we worried about the environment. Everyone agrees global warming should be stopped, and if it isn't, Anchorage will soon look like Miami.

I have also dealt with creationsim versus Darwinism. Did God create the earth in six days, or did we originate from monkeys? I discuss this because a book that mentions God sells more copies to human beings than one that appeals to apes.

I also deal with the Iraq war. It is not my position that it was a good war or a bad war, a just war or an unjust war, a smart war or the dumbest war we have ever gotten into. My position is that it is the only war we've got, so we have to support it.

Do you want to know how I feel about torture? Personally, I am against it, but if we can get information out of someone by breaking his knuckles, attaching electrodes to his testicles, or dragging him around with a dog leash, I say go for it—unless it violates the Geneva Convention. Then you do it in the kitchen where no one can see you.

Does this book appeal to conservatives or liberals? It appeals to both. There is something in it for anyone who watches Fox News, agrees with Bill O'Reilly and thinks Rush Limbaugh is a really neat guy. The reason I say this is because conservatives buy books. Ann Coulter is the right wing's answer to Al Franken's wife. All the liberals have are Michael Moore and Hillary Clinton—and we all know about them. But that doesn't mean I don't stick up for the Left. They buy books too (using food stamps).

There is something for everyone on the political spectrum.

You don't have to be a "born again" anything. You don't even have to be in favor of the Ten Commandments on state capitol buildings.

Some people may try to stop this book from being published because it makes fun of our president and all our revered institutions, including McDonald's golden arches. But this is a free country, and you can write anything you want to. Getting on the best-seller list is another story.

Introduction

BY GARRY TRUDEAU

....

I'VE ALWAYS BEEN PARTIAL to introductions—particularly considering the alternative. If you need no introduction whatsoever, you're probably paying some terrible price. Think Kato Kaelin. Martha Stewart. Paris Hilton. You get the idea.

There are, of course, happy exceptions: For many years, Art Buchwald needed no introduction. If he paid a price, I am unaware of it. I'm only aware of people paying him. In fact, he still needs no introduction to two generations of keenly devoted readers. (You folks can proceed directly to Chapter One.) It's the newest generation that's got him worried, and it should, because the young don't seem to read newspapers, which is where both of us ply our trade. That Mr. Buchwald's publisher has turned to me to bridge this gap is touching, because like the author, I've been handing out the same publicity photo for twenty years, effectively freezing the aging process, at least in the public imagination.

In any event, I'm happy to play along, because like most people in the satire biz, I am in Buchwald's debt, with no hope of ever retiring it. His influence has been so wide and pervasive that all of us who make our livings with peashooters and slingshots and mud pies regard him with awe and, of course, suspicion. No one human, we reason, no matter how ambitious, could possibly strike so many blows in so many deserving quarters on such a consistent basis. There must be a team—Team Buchwald—assembling his columns. The maestro probably writes the lead and names his "source" (usually someone like "my pal Smeadley at Foggy Bottom"), but after that it's outsourced to Tegucigalpa, where humble but wily campesinos, raised on badly-dubbed episodes of *The Simpsons*, cobble together the main text in comedy sweatshops so poorly lit that they must work in braille. The raw column is then translated back into standard English and returned to the head office on Connecticut Avenue where it is burnished by senior stylists for Buchwald's final approval.

It's just a theory. But in its absence, there is simply no explanation for Buchwald's half century of carrying on so magnificently without pause. Woody Allen is right that 80 percent of success is showing up—and Art has shown up longer (about 92 percent longer), and with greater panache and good cheer (110 percent more), than anyone currently practicing the black arts.

If this is all news to you, great. Consider yourself introduced. Take it away, Art.

Economics Lesson

"ALL RIGHT CLASS, today we're going to discuss the economic factors that make a society work. To make it easier, the children whose parents have jobs will sit on this side of the room. Those whose mothers and fathers don't have jobs, sit on that side.

"Now, in order to have a successful economy you have to have money. Most people earn their money by having a job. You get paid by the company for services rendered, such as working for a telephone company, or being a computer programmer. Now, as soon as Alfred Sidewinder is paid, he gives the money to someone else, like a department store or the grocer, usually with a credit card.

"The department store or the grocer then takes Alfred's money and puts it in the bank to pay off their own debts. The bank, in turn, lends the money to Howard Simpan, who wants to buy a house, and to Frederick Lipscomb, who wants to open a pizza

21

parlor. In a good economy, everybody is handing each other money, and everyone is happy. Some invest money in stocks, and these companies then spread the wealth because everyone believes the market will always go up.

"That's the good side. The bad side is, if Alfred Sidewinder, at the beginning of the merry-go-round, doesn't spend any money. Then we have a recession."

One of the children on the side of the unemployed parents says, "My father doesn't have any money. He lost his job making office file cabinets." Another one yells, "My father lost his job as an airline pilot." A third one chimes in, "My father has no work because his greeting card company printed all their cards in Indonesia."

A child on the side of the room whose parents are still working says, "My father won't let my mother spend any money. He says you never know when you will no longer have a job."

"If the economy gets better will the people get their jobs back?" a child asks.

"That's an interesting question. The only way to get out of a recession is to have the people working again. Many companies are laying off workers because they say they aren't making any money. They have no intention of hiring them back because they realized how much they would save if they had half their employees."

"What's the answer?"

"President Bush thinks a tax cut for large companies should do the job."

"What about Christmas?" someone asks.

"That's a good point. It could be a good year or a bad year, depending on Sidewinder. The ball is in his court now. It would be nice if the children on the unemployed side of the room could soon be sitting on the other side. But it will happen only after the economy hits bottom. Are there any questions?"

Trouble in the Middle East

AS IF WE DIDN'T HAVE ENOUGH trouble in the Middle East, the Saudi Arabians are now suing the American tobacco companies to compensate for twenty-five years of their government treating smoking-related illnesses. (No joke.)

Ahmed al-Tuwaijri, lawyer for the King Faisal Hospital, called the suit part of a "holy war" against the tobacco interests, as if the U.S. needed another "holy war" at this time. He called tobacco "The biggest corruption on earth."

I don't think Mr. Al-Tuwaijri has been reading the papers lately.

Saudi Arabia is the fourth largest importer of American tobacco in the world, and since treatment in Saudi hospitals is free, the government is making the tobacco companies eat sand.

So now the U.S. has a serious problem on its hands. Does the United States take the side of the American tobacco industry because it brings in so many dollars, or do they prepare for a "Tobacco Jihad?"

It's a tough choice because the Saudi Arabians have been known to walk a mile for a Camel. Since they can't drink, the only thing they can do is puff away to their hearts' content.

No one knows what Saudi Arabians would do if you took away their butts. While the hospital is asking for three billion dollars to pay for people who have smoking illnesses, the tobacco companies say it's not their fault. They are just making people happy.

The anti-smoking forces in the U.S. who are allied with those in Saudi Arabia have suggested that the entire country become a smoke-free zone, and anyone who lights up should be publicly flogged.

The big fear is that other Middle Eastern countries will follow suit. Since that area is one of the biggest markets, the tobacco companies must speak softly but carry a big stick. To make sure the playing field is not level, the suit is being pursued in the Grand Islamic court in Riyadh. Phillip Morris is not sure they can find twelve just men.

An American tobacco company representative, who shall remain nameless, said, "If they won't buy our cigarettes we won't buy their oil."

"That should scare them," I said.

"We have to be able to export our product overseas because there is so much pressure here from American anti-smoking zealots."

An interesting statistic is that 40 percent of all Saudi men smoke and 10 percent of all Saudi women—though this last figure would be higher if we knew who was smoking under their burkas.

God Bless

THERE ARE SO MANY PEOPLE to thank this Christmas. I don't know where to begin. First, I would like to thank the People's Sweat Shop of Shanghai for the beautiful American flag glove and scarf set, which makes me feel very patriotic.

To the Taiwan Watch Factory, who made it possible for me to have a knock-off of a Rolex, I send my appreciation. No one could tell the difference and it only cost $19.50. (The one with diamonds cost $29.95.)

And I don't want to forget the luggage with the Stars and Stripes on it, made in Child Labor Factory Number 4 in the Philippines. It looks exactly like a real Louis Vuitton, and even has a lifetime guarantee.

My gratitude to the government inspectors in Sri Lanka. The tennis shoes with an American flag stenciled on them were a size seven and I'm an eleven. I am sending them back. I thank you for letting me exchange them.

I would also like to thank the woman in Nepal for the cashmere sweaters on which she knitted "God Bless America." If you bought one you got one free, so my wife now has two.

And, lest we forget it, I'll always be grateful for the Bavarian cuckoo clock from Korea that plays "My Country 'Tis of Thee" on the hour. Please wish all the prisoners who worked on it in Seoul Prison Number 1348 my best regards.

There are so many people I'd like to thank for making my holiday such a great one.

The toy U.S. Marines from Bombay, India, were a hit with my grandson, and he hasn't stopped playing with them.

And the female naval flying officer doll was a smash with my granddaughter. Another big hit was a dancing Santa Claus holding an American flag in his hand made by the Hutus in Madagascar. Everyone loves it.

Unfortunately, the Mother Soon Wong fruitcake from Hong Kong arrived smashed, but we're not blaming Mother Soon Wong. She didn't know it was being sent through the U.S. Postal Service.

It's amazing how many individuals can contribute to one's Christmas. The people who make these products are as happy as those who received them. Did I tell you about the prescription drugs I got from Tijuana, Mexico? My wife wrapped them in a beautiful box that read, "Take 50 percent off tagged price."

I did get a wrapped bottle of men's cologne called "America's Best," with "Made in the USA" printed on it. I asked the family, "How did this get in here? We better open it in the garage."

Saving Time

PEOPLE ARE NOW EXPECTED to arrive at the airport at least two hours before takeoff due to security precautions. Once you go through the metal detector, what do you do to kill time?

Here are some suggestions. If you're married, pick up on the argument you were having at home. It's also a good time to ask your husband if he shut off the gas jets on the stove. And your husband can wonder if the parakeet will be safe with the neighbors. Or alternately, sit there for two hours without talking to each other.

If you are a person who is traveling with someone who is not your wife, buy her a box of See's candy. Tell her what a wonderful time she is going to have in Disney World, where nobody will know the two of you.

If you are a divorced woman, tell him your ex was a rat who never took you to Disney World in all the years you were married. Tell him you usually don't eat candy, but in his case you'll make an exception. If both of you are unattached, you may hold hands in the terminal. If one is married and the other isn't, one of you should sit at Gate 40 and the other at Gate 29, pretending you don't know each other.

When a girl looks as if she is alone and you feel like flirting, ask her if you didn't meet her in Chicago. If she says no, try

Albuquerque, or Alaska. If she is bored and you look respectable, she will start talking.

If it's a guy and he is by himself, the girl can say something like, "I noticed your argyle socks when security made you take off your shoes, and they are gorgeous."

No one is going to be hurt, and you might even find Mr. Right or Ms. Right if you are taking the same flight.

Plane-waiting may also mean being alert and watching everyone in the air terminal to guess whether they are terrorists or not. You may decide one person fits the profile of Osama bin Laden or one of his henchmen. Anyone who looks suspicious should be followed during his time at the gate.

One pleasure of waiting is reading all the magazines at the newsstand your parents won't let you read at home. For boys it could be *Penthouse* or *Playboy*, and for girls, *Sex and Getting Your Man in a Week*. My favorite is *Cosmopolitan*. It doesn't pull any punches. It's the magazine that lets it all hang out.

There is nothing more tantalizing than food at an airport. Caution—don't drink more than six cups of coffee before taking off. You can eat all the pizza you want, but limit yourself to five Whoppers.

The most dangerous place at the airport is the bar. It's a question of how much booze you can consume in two hours, particularly if you're buying a stranger a drink and he is reciprocating beer for beer. Do not discuss politics, football, or even religion.

Warning—the worst thing you can do while waiting is make friends with someone else's child. Once the kid discovers you're a patsy, he will drive you crazy. No matter how cute they look, remember, they're a pain in the neck to somebody.

These are just a few ways to wait in the airport. They were given to me by frequent flyers who know the ropes.

Waiting is now more fun than flying, except if security makes you take off your clothes.

Let's Not Forget the Lobbyists

ENRON'S DIFFICULTIES not only gave us a lesson in Economics 101, but they also explained how Washington operates.

Everyone in Enron played his role—from the executives in the company and their accounting firm, to the lawyers who served them so well. But none of them could accomplish what they did without the Washington lobbyists. They are the ones who protect companies from a government that cannot be trusted.

Lobbyists are just like you and me—they put on their golf shoes one foot at a time. But you have to be qualified to be a lobbyist. Many, if not all, are recruited from Congress. They have decided they are fed up with politics and want to make some big money for a change, or have lost an election and are not fit to do anything else.

Lobbyists are very friendly people. They call lawmakers and administration officials by their first names: "Ted," "Terry," and "George." Theirs is the only profession, except for the FBI, that makes house calls.

The job of the lobbyist is to stop a law that will hurt his clients and lobby for a bill that will make everyone rich.

This is an example of how it works. The Hidden Valley Gas and Power Company has ex-Senator Glad Handle on its payroll to lobby for them in Washington. Glad Handle is a Republican, and he replaced ex-Congressman Taylor Bluewhistle, a Democrat, who was fired after Al Gore lost the election.

Glad moves between the Capitol, the White House, and any agency that can affect Hidden Valley business.

Let's say Congress wants to pass a law forbidding Hidden Valley from delivering natural gas and smoking cigarettes at the same time.

What Congress doesn't know is that Hidden Valley owns a cigarette company as well as a gas company. Banning smoking near a gas plant will seriously hurt their tobacco business.

Glad invites Senator Carl Fiddle to Burning Tree Country club. Fiddle is in charge of the Smoking and Energy Committee. He is greeted warmly by Handle, who says, "Remember when we filibustered an equal rights bill together?"

They play eighteen holes and then Glad asks Fiddle, "How's the election campaign going?"

"We could use $100,000 in soft money to buy sweatshirts for our volunteers."

Glad takes out his checkbook and says, "Why didn't you say that before?"

Senator Fiddle replies, "You're a lobbyist, so we hated to ask you for something. If we take your money what can we do for you?"

"Nothing much. If you want to hold up the Anti-Smoking Gas bill in committee, that would be fun."

"It's done."

"What about getting the oil rights to West Point?" Glad asks.

"I know the person at EPA you should ask for."

Glad says, "Can I buy you a beer?"

"You know, Glad, that's against Senate rules."

Which God Is Your God?

THE ARGUMENT STARTED late at night in a bar, where most arguments begin.

Cornblatt said, "I wish to God I didn't have to go home tonight."

Rutherford said, "There is no God."

And suddenly all of us were off and running.

I asked Rutherford if he was an atheist and he denied it. He said, "I don't believe there is no God, I believe there are too many gods."

George, the bartender, was happy to serve us all drinks, as it was a slow night.

"And what in God's name does that mean?" I asked.

Rutherford said, "Everyone in the world seems to have a god, and that's alright until they want to kill other people who have a different god. Look what's going on in the Moslem world. They call people in the Western world infidels and are willing to fight a Holy War to satisfy their god."

"Those are only the terrorists," Cornblatt said, "and it's costing us billions of dollars to protect our God."

Rutherford asked, "What do you mean, 'our God?' Depending on our faiths, there are dozens of gods that we worship. Take Ireland, for example. The Protestant Irish have been killing the Catholic believers, and the Catholics have been murdering the Protestants. They are all the same people, except for their religion. If they can't agree on who is the real God, how can anybody else?"

George, the bartender, tried to protect his bottles because he didn't know where this was going.

Pearlstein, who was trying to stay out of the argument, said, "The Jewish religion has the true God, and that is why we are the Chosen People."

"You may be, except Orthodox Jews don't believe in what the Conservative Jews and the Reformed Jews stand for. They have an entirely different idea of what God thinks about women."

Pearlstein said, "If we had been proselytizing back in 1300 BC like the other religions do now, the whole world would be Jewish."

Cornblatt said, "When I was a kid I always asked God for something. He helped me if I didn't do my homework or if I had a difficult test—and even when I asked for help after disobeying my parents. Every time I asked a favor I told Him, 'I'll never ask you for anything again.'"

I said, "There was a bully at our school named Sam Tufano, and after school he would chase me. I asked God to make me run faster than Tufano, and He never let me down."

George said, "It's time to close up—no more drinks."

It was a good idea because we were just about to discuss God and the Jehovah's Witnesses.

Yesterday's Enemy

I WALKED PAST the Soviet Embassy the other day after President Bush made his State of the Union Speech.

Over the years the Soviet Embassy was one of the most vilified buildings in Washington—and the most mistrusted.

There were several U.S. Secret Service cars in front of the embassy at all times. The FBI rented apartments across the street for its cameras and listening equipment. The CIA even built a tunnel from a house on a hill that went right into the embassy. We listened to everything that Moscow was plotting.

All a president had to do to get a standing ovation in Congress was call the Soviet Union the "Evil Empire."

When criticized for our spy community's vigilance, the State Department replied, "All is fair in love and the Cold War."

I ran into Davidson, who takes the same walk every morning as I do. I said, "It's pretty quiet around here."

"It wouldn't be if Bush had blasted the Russkies in his speech."

I asked, "Is it politically correct to call them Russkies now?"

"What would you call them?"

"Our brave allies beyond the Iron Curtain."

"But what happened to the days when we said the Russians were stocking nuclear arms and we had no choice but to do the same? That is why the president needs $200 billion for a new missile shield. The only enemies mentioned in Mr. Bush's speech were North Korea, Iran and Iraq."

I said, "The president should have said he needs the money to prevent the Russians from smuggling nuclear weapons in battered suitcases."

"What made the Reds such an easy target for a State of the Union speech in the old days was that nothing in their country worked, and it was always cold."

"We had a real enemy in those days. All we have now are faceless terrorists who will never have an embassy of their own because just before they open one they commit suicide."

Davidson said, "I used to be afraid of Russian spies who hung out beyond those walls. Now when I see one on the street I imagine he is either a defector or someone going to the Safeway to buy a *National Enquirer.*"

"How did the Russians become the number one good guys so soon after they were the number one bad guys?"

"It is easy, because Bush can get Vladimir Putin on the phone anytime he wants to—but Osama bin Laden never returns his calls."

Dinner at the Darbys'

I WAS HAVING DINNER at the Darbys' when Sheila Darby said, "Guess what Caroline wants to be when she grows up?"

We all looked at Caroline, who is sixteen years old. She said, 'I want to be a whistleblower."

"That's an honorable profession," I said. "But you have to work hard to catch a person who is up to no good."

"That's what I told her," her father, Joe, said. "You have fifteen minutes of glory and then you can't find a job."

Caroline said, "Sherron Watkins of Enron is my role model. All the girls at school think she is fantastic."

I said, "Whistleblowers have come into their own ever since Sherron spilled the beans. But no one at Enron backed her up. Whistleblowing is a very lonely business."

Joe said, "I don't want TV cameras on my lawn all day and all night."

Caroline said, "That's the part I like the most. I could be interviewed on the *Today Show,* and *Good Morning America,* and by

Tom Brokaw. He could say I was a member of the Greatest Generation."

Sheila said to Caroline, "If you're going to be a whistleblower you're going to need a decent education. No one is going to believe you if you don't have a college degree."

Joe said, "There are corporate whistleblowers who report on their bosses stealing from the pension fund. No one in the company will talk to them at the water cooler anymore."

Caroline asked, "How do I practice being a whistleblower?"

I suggested, "For starters, you could snitch on your fourteen-year-old brother Tommy."

Caroline said, "I saw him smoking a cigarette outside Tyson's Corner mall."

I said to the Darbys, "She's a natural whistleblower."

Tommy was angry and yelled at Caroline, "I was not and you know it!"

Joe said, "If I were you, Tommy, I'd take the Fifth Amendment."

Caroline said, "By the time I grow up, Sherron Watkins will have used up her 15 minutes."

I replied, "Not necessarily. Don't forget she has a book to write and her story will be made into a TV movie."

Joe complained, "That means we'll have to give up all our privacy. Sherron Watkins may be a very successful whistle-blower, but there are thousands of tattle-tales whom you have never heard about. They lost their jobs and their health insurance."

Sheila said, "I like what Caroline wants to do. If she can find a crooked accountant or a smarmy lawyer to rat out when she grows up we should encourage her."

Tommy said, "I would rather be a crooked accountant. You make more money."

Caroline told him, "If you were, I would send you to jail."

Tommy retorted, "Says who?"

I interrupted and said, "I would rather have a whistleblower than a crooked lawyer in the family."

Sheila said, "Wouldn't we all?"

Book Flogging

I FLEW DOWN to the Broward Public Library in Fort Lauderdale, Florida to do a book signing for a paperback I wrote.

Over the years I have done thousands of book-signings (well anyhow, quite a few). It's even tougher than writing a book. Sandy Vanocur once told me, "You know you've been on the road too long when you've run out of quarters for the vibrating bed in your motel."

I have had many adventures in my book-signing career. One of my favorites was when I went to a department store in Rochester. The books were set up in the lobby. By accident I received a copy of the instructions for the staff.

One employee was assigned to make sure the books were there. Another supplied the ice water. A third person was in charge of supplying the pens.

The last assignment on the list had to do with security. Written next to it was the notation, "Mr. Buchwald does not need security because he is not that well-known."

When you're flogging a book you sit in a lot of TV show Green Rooms, waiting to go on the air. I shared one in Chicago with a chimpanzee that was holding on to his owner for dear life. I kept eyeing the chimp, and he kept eyeing me. Finally, his owner, a little old lady, asked me to hold him while she changed his diaper. At that moment I declared I was going to give up show business.

Sometimes on the road you are the victim of a breaking story, and they tell you they are going to bounce you off the air.

This happened in Detroit. A friend, Tony Kornheiser, was with me plugging his book. The producer came out and said, "We have to cancel both of you. We just invaded Grenada."

I immediately said, "I just came back from Grenada."

He said, "Then come on the air."

When the producer left the room, Tony growled, "You lying SOB. You don't even know where Grenada is."

I said, "You have to think fast when you are out on the road."

Jim Michener and I were good friends, though he outsold me in the bookstores by one hundred to one.

One time I was at a bookstore on Fifth Avenue for an autograph session. Michener's *Hawaii* was displayed all over the window. My book was hidden all the way in the back.

I took off my suit jacket and looked for someone who worked there. I called over a stockroom boy and said, "You see all those Michener books in the window? Put them in the back and take the books in the back and put them in the window." It was one of my greatest book-signing triumphs, and when I told him, Michener laughed and said he was wondering why everyone was going to the back of the store.

The toughest book-signing competitor I ever had was Sylvia Porter, the business author and columnist. I appeared with her at a book luncheon. She talked about bonds and I talked about Washington. After we both spoke, we signed books. I had two people (my sisters) waiting to buy my book, and Sylvia Porter had a line that went around the block.

I learned from Andy Rooney that the only way to speed up a book-signing line is not to talk to anyone whose book you are autographing.

That is what I did in Fort Lauderdale. Flogging one's book is a dirty business, but somebody has to do it.

Shadow Government

AS YOU READ THIS COLUMN, there is a "shadow government" somewhere in the bowels of the mountains of Maryland, where people are stationed to keep the country going in case of nuclear war. I'm not sure how long these officials have to remain underground, but it is the toughest job in the country.

This is what it must be like:

The officials are having dinner in their cave.

Marty Muggeridge says, "I am supposed to be the shadow president this week."

Hal Haige says, "It's my turn. You were president last week."

"No one ever lets me be president," Gonbalt says. "I'm tired of being the shadow environmental Cabinet officer."

Hogan, the standby homeland security director says, "I want everyone to be stripped before I allow them into the cave."

The standby attorney general says, "I want to practice military tribunals, just in case. If I ever have to be the real AG, I'm going to take away all the people's rights."

While they are eating, Artie Bear, the backup secretary of defense, comes in the room and says tearfully, "Someone has been sleeping in my bed."

The ersatz secretary of the treasury says, "And someone was eating out of my bowl."

The substitute secretary of state says, "Someone has been sitting in my chair."

The stand-in attorney general says, "This is a case for the FBI."

The surrogate CIA head chimes in, "We have a tip that it is Goldilocks, the shadow secretary of labor."

The substitute AG says, "Let's round up anyone in the cave who looks suspicious."

Nancy Hubbard, the backup national security director says, "I went to the cupboard this morning and it was bare."

The alternate OMB director says, "There was nothing in the budget for the cupboard. You should have stocked it with pork."

One of the shadow White House officials says, "We're not supposed to do anything until the balloon goes up. But there is no reason why we can't practice damage control."

"How can we have spin if we don't have a press secretary?"

"I'm here," a man at the end of the table says. "I can give you all the spin you want."

As the shadow men and women are talking, someone enters the cave. The secretary of defense asks the secretary of state, "Who is that?"

"Beats me. I never saw him before in my life."

The shadow homeland security director says, "I better keep an eye on him."

The pseudo-secretary of agriculture says, "He looks exactly like Vice President Cheney."

It *is* Vice President Cheney," the substitute secretary of the treasury says.

"Then what is he doing down here?"

The CIA man replies, "They want him out of sight, and what better place than with the shadow government?"

Haige says, "If the real vice president is here, then I can't be the shadow vice president."

"You can be the shadow secretary of commerce."

Haige says, "I'm always getting the wrong end of the stick."

Safe Deposit for Sale

SOME OF THE LARGEST and most patriotic American companies are incorporating in the Caribbean to avoid paying income taxes. Billions of dollars are being deposited in such places as the Cayman Islands and Bermuda.

The slogan for the companies is: "Our stockholders, right or wrong."

There is such a rush on overseas deposit boxes that they are sought after by everyone. As soon as one becomes available, every self-respecting tax evader bids on it.

Here are some of the top boxes now being advertised:

"A beautiful safe deposit box, overlooking the blue waters of Turtle Reef. Enough room for a million dollars' worth of tax-free cash or bonds. Perfect for someone who is just starting out in business."

Another ad reads, "This box is located in one of the largest banks on Grand Cayman Island. It originally housed offshore money from the Enron Company. A steal since the company went bankrupt. It is more than a deposit box—it is a room with its own laundromat for laundering tax money worth more than $10 million. The room comes in mahogany, and has two sets of electric locks, just like the ones at the Federal Reserve."

This is a good one: "For the first time, this safe with three rooms and nuclear bomb-proof walls is for sale. It was put on the market by a motion picture company that sent all its worldwide receipts to the Cayman Islands in hopes of saving $100 million a year in taxes.

"Rodney Murthless, president of the company, said, 'We had to do it because our two blockbusters turned out to be turkeys. We were sorry to give it up because the box also came with golf privileges and a marina, which our executives and movie stars used when they flew in from Hollywood.'"

This one appeared in the want ads: "Attention certified accountants. Your clients deserve only the best, which means they need protection from the IRS. We now have condominium safes that are located in the peaceful sand dunes, away from the hustle and bustle of town. If you sign up you will automatically become a member of the Cayman Tax Cheaters Club. Safe deposit boxes start at $80,000, and our lawyers will do your corporate paperwork for you. Your box will have a confidential number that the FBI will never be able to track down.

"Speaking of condos, the Caymans are now offering time-share safes for two-week periods. The choice time to do this is in April, when you want to be near your money."

What's good about putting your money in an offshore account is that the administration hasn't said anything against it. One of the reasons is that the Bush administration smiles on the rich people and makes sure they get all the breaks.

I know one company that hangs the U.S. flag from the roof of its building, buys Girl Scout cookies, supports political candidates, but prefers to be incorporated in the beautiful islands offshore.

The CEO of the company said, "We not only don't pay any taxes, but we hope to get rebates from the IRS to put us in the black."

I asked a banker if ordinary citizens in lower income brackets could go offshore. He said, "Offshore is only for the big guys who can't stand pain."

The Young Audience

EVERY TIME I PICK UP the papers I read that a network is bragging about one of its shows attracting the 18-to-39-year-old audience. And why shouldn't they brag?

The 18-to-39s are the only ones in America who have any buying power. The network producer of a reality show called *Death Rattle* told me *Death* was watched by 40 million people, all under the age of 40. The person who doesn't die from a heart attack after climbing Mount Everest wins a million dollars.

Ron Kendall, the producer, was merciless. "We are reaching the audience we want and we are making the sponsor very happy. The 18-to-39-year-old audience buys beer, Nike running shoes and BMWs. They are making the economy soar, unlike the tightwad 40-to-90-year-old losers who hang on to their money because they are afraid their pensions won't get them through their September years."

I said: "But the biggest advertisers on television are the drug companies, which are selling pharmaceuticals for everything from arthritis to insomnia."

"At the moment these are not problems of the 39-and-under crowd," Kendall told me. "But they will be later. All the drug companies are trying to do at this time is educate the younger people as to what they have to look forward to later on. We want the kids to know when they turn 40, and for the rest of their lives, they will always have Viagra waiting for them."

I asked, "Suppose the over-40 population wants to buy something?"

"We can't stop them. At the same time, the advertiser is not sucking up to them."

"What does that mean?"

"Well, our surveys show that the mature audiences always go to the washroom when the commercial comes on, and they take a newspaper with them."

"Where do the 18-to-39s get their money?" I asked.

"From their parents. One of the reasons the over-40s are lacking in purchasing power is that they have to support their children."

"Even the 39-year-olds?"

"Especially the 39-year-olds."

"Are all your shows aimed at the youth market?"

"Of course," he said. "The networks are always trying to put no-brainers on the air. The less complicated the program is, the higher the rating."

"Is *Death Rattle* so popular because you don't have to be a nuclear scientist to understand it?"

"You can say that again."

Suddenly, two men came into Kendall's office and started

removing furniture. "What are you doing?" Kendall asked them. One of the movers read from a slip of paper.

"You're Ron Kendall and you were born in 1962. That makes you 40 and you have been fired."

"Give me a break. I didn't know about this."

"You should have thought of that before you decided to turn 40."

It's Cherry Blossom Time

SPRING IS THE MOST BEAUTIFUL time of the year in Washington. It is cherry blossom time. In past years, tourists from all over the world came to look at the blossoms. But now it's different, because the cherry blossoms are looking at us. As part of Homeland Security, video cameras have been placed in the trees and monuments around the Tidal Basin.

There is now an FBI Cherry Blossom SWAT Team whose sole job it is to monitor tourists who go in and out of the Tidal Basin.

The team is located in the cellar of the J. Edgar Hoover building, where they man the TV screens 24 hours a day.

Let's see where it all leads. Two of the agents are studying the screens.

"Buck, I think I've got someone standing under the Weeping Higan tree by the Lincoln Memorial."

"Which one?"

"The guy in the red jersey with the New York Yankees baseball cap. He's taking a picture of his wife and two kids who are eating salt-water taffy."

"I see them now. What makes you think they could be terrorists?"

"Why would someone be taking pictures of the cherry blossoms unless he had a subversive reason? I'm going to do a visual recognition on him."

The agent went to his computer. He put the tourist's picture on the screen and the computer started spitting out information. The agent read, "He's Brad Ellicott, a lawyer who lives in Greenwich with his wife and two children. He went to Harvard, she to Wellesley. Ellicott is a rock-ribbed Republican and gave $100 to Bush in the last election. He has no known connection to any terrorist organizations except the ACLU. Well, we have nothing there."

The other agent says, "Look over there at the Capitol. You see the demonstrator with the sign protesting the high cost of prescription drugs?"

"The guy looks seventy years old. He's shouting that drug companies are sticking it to the people who need the drugs the most."

"He sounds like an agitator to me. Let's do a profile on him. My gosh, listen to this. He studied psychology at Berkeley, was a member of the Socialist Party, voted for Adlai Stevenson, and subscribed to the *Nation* magazine. He spent a year in Europe where he hung out with Ernest Hemingway and Jean-Paul Sartre. He was always a troublemaker."

The first agent said, "We better find out what he is really up to." He pushed the Homeland Security button and a SWAT team came roaring out of the basement, their sirens blaring.

As the agents watched on the TV monitor, the SWAT team tore down the protestor's sign and body-searched him. Then the lieutenant called the FBI at Cherry Blossom Headquarters and said, "We found nothing except an unfilled prescription for $200 arthritis pills."

Malice on Purpose

I JUST READ THAT SATIRE could be dangerous to your health. Two officials in Texas are suing a weekly newspaper for printing a story that a reporter wrote. It was a satirical piece, which pretended the officials had sent a six-year-old to prison for reading a book in class. The basis of the satire was that a judge and a district attorney had actually sent a thirteen-year-old to jail. The plaintiffs claimed they were libeled because the story was not labeled satire.

This scared the heck out of me because satire is my business and I can't afford to defend myself—particularly at the prices lawyers charge these days.

Let me give you an example of how satire works.

I read where the Republicans sent out invitations for a fundraiser in Washington. In the invitation was a letter saying donors could also buy three patriotic photos of the president taken on 9/11, which they could have as souvenirs for $150 extra.

Now this is the kind of story I love because it makes you realize how tacky politics can really be.

I interviewed a Republican fundraiser (fictitious, of course), accusing him of cashing in on what was one of the saddest days in our history, and he replied, "It wasn't political—it was patriotic. Besides, President Clinton did a lot worse. For a fee he let his guests leave their dirty socks in the Lincoln Bedroom." (I am bringing the Democrats into it to give the Republican side, which is a brilliant idea.)

He added, "The only ones who think the photo idea was smarmy were the left-wing liberals who are critical of anything the president does." (That's what we in the satire business call a "zinger.")

I said, "Some critics say the Republican fundraisers are sucking up to the right wing."

He said, "Why shouldn't we? They were the ones who got Bush elected." (Bull's-eye.)

The question, dear reader, is how someone can be fair if he writes satire. The answer is, he can't. Satire is malicious, and until now, protected by the First Amendment.

It is a way to express an opinion and also make the reader laugh. The important thing is for the person reading to have knowledge of what is being satirized so he/she can be in on the joke.

I remember once during the McCarthy days I wrote an article saying that almost every town in America had four or five organizations to fight communists—but the towns didn't have any communists. I suggested each one import a communist to come there and be the threat. He would throw garbage on people's lawns, demonstrate at the courthouse and agree to have his phone tapped by the FBI.

The column caused a tremendous reaction, some negative, some positive, but I think I made my point.

We live in a country where writers can satirize anything they want to, even their own satire.

It's a malicious business, but someone has to do it.

Red Alert

....

LIKE MOST AMERICANS, I listen to what my leaders tell me to do. So when Cheney of the White House, Rumsfeld of Defense, Ridge of Homeland Security and Ashcroft of Justice tell me to prepare for an attack, I listen.

The next question I ask myself is, if we are attacked, what do I do? Certainly Homeland Security has plans for me.

I called the Homeland Security hotline and told the man who answered the phone, "I have heard the alert warnings and I want to get out of town."

"Where do you live?"

"Washington, D.C., right near American University."

He said, "That's a bad place to be in case of an attack."

"I know that. Could you advise me on how to escape from the area?"

"Take the Beltway."

"But isn't everyone else taking the Beltway?"

There was a pause. "Maybe you're right. Take the Bay Bridge in Maryland and drive until you hit the Perdue Chicken Ranch, and hide in a hatchery until the all-clear is sounded."

"It's pretty hard to get on the bridge on a normal weekend, much less during an alert. I'll be in my car for 10 hours and then run out of gas."

He said, "You are not being helpful. Suppose you took the subway to Reagan National Airport and grabbed a plane."

"Where to?"

"Buffalo is as good as anyplace. At least it's not a prime target."

"That is a big help."

"Don't forget North Carolina. Nobody is going to blow up Nags Head."

"How do I get from Washington to Nags Head?"

"Call the AAA. They'll tell you."

"Is this a red alert or a green one?"

"It's a red one, which means fill up your gas tank, put a dozen bottles of water in the back seat, and carry antacid pills."

"What about my credit cards?"

"Be sure to take them with you. There may be a lot of places along the line where you can use them."

"Where are you going to be?"

"In the mountains of West Virginia. Since I am one of the top people in Homeland Security, they are going to fly me out in a helicopter."

"I gotcha. Suppose I stay in the basement?"

"Good idea. When we find where the threat is, I'll call you back."

"One last question. I know I should be on the alert, but what should I be alert for?"

"That's the FBI's secret."

The FBI Changes Its Ways

EVEN THOUGH J. EDGAR HOOVER is turning over in his grave, the FBI is changing its ways. The priority now is terrorism, and crime may be on the back burner. This is what could happen:

"Is this the FBI?"

"It's not Pizza Hut."

"I have a tip for you. I just saw John Dillinger, the notorious bank robber, enter a movie with a redhead. He looked armed and dangerous."

"We don't do bank robbers anymore. Did you notice if he had any explosives in his shoes?"

"He might have. I just wanted to alert you."

"Look, mister, if we had to tie up our agents with bank-robbing cases, we'd never find out where Osama bin Laden is hanging out. Call back in a couple of weeks and if Dillinger is still with the redhead, let us know."

"Is this the FBI?"

"All our lines are busy. Please wait for the next available agent. Your call is very important to us and will be taped for our files."

Twenty-five minutes later someone answers the phone.

"FBI. I can't talk to you about drugs because we've reduced our drug department to two undercover agents in Mexico."

"This is Senator Boogle. One of my constituents was appointed to the Global Warming Committee last year, and he still hasn't been cleared by the FBI."

"We don't have time to clear people in the government. He will have to wait his turn like everybody else."

"How long will that be?"

"If he's lucky, we should finish our paperwork by 2006."

The phone rings again. "Mr. Hanssen, the traitor, is unable to come to the phone. He is either in solitary or being squeezed dry by our agents."

Next call: "Have you given any executives at Enron lie detector tests, since they have certainly committed criminal acts?"

"The FBI has gone out of the white-collar crime business."

"Suppose I told you some of their people are terrorists."

"No kidding. We'll get on their case right away."

"Am I speaking to the Federal Bureau of Investigation?"

"Yes."

"I just saw Bonnie and Clyde."

"So?"

"They were taking flying lessons in Minneapolis."

"Everybody takes flying lessons in Minneapolis."

The changeover in the bureau is proceeding faster than anyone thought it would. The phones are being manned at all times. One of the most interesting changes is that the FBI has taken the CIA off its most-wanted list. One of the major ones is that the FBI is accepting calls from whistleblowers. This is something Hoover would never have agreed to.

Declaration

THIS DIDN'T HAPPEN, but it could have. In 1776 the American Colonies had decided to break off from the British. It looked like war and everyone was frightened because each side had so many fearful blunderbusses in its arsenal.

King George decided to send over Sir Duncan Rumsfeld, his minister of defense.

Rumsfeld met with Thomas Jefferson at his home in Virginia.

"It's good to see you," Sir Duncan said. "We're all in mourning because Britain lost the World Cup."

Jefferson said, "What brings you to these beleaguered states?"

Sir Duncan said, "Mr. Jefferson—why do your colonies want

to separate from Britain? You have a good life, we buy your tobacco, and King George III loves you very much."

Jefferson replied, "The History of the present King of Great-Britain is a History of repeated Injuries and Usurpations, all having in direct Object the Establishment of an absolute Tyranny over these States. How do you spell 'tyranny'?"

"I think it's T-I-Y-R-A-N-N-I-E."

Jefferson kept reading from his notes. "He has quartered large Bodies of Armed Troops among us, protecting them by a mock Trial, from Punishment for any Murders which they should commit on the Inhabitants of these States.

"He has plundered our Seas, ravaged our Coasts, burnt our Towns, and destroyed the Lives of our People."

Sir Duncan said: "Everyone makes mistakes. Colonies are always complaining about how their rulers treat them. Make a list of your so-called gripes, and I'll take them back to London."

Jefferson continued: "He is, at this Time, transporting large Armies of foreign Mercenaries to compleat the Works of Death, of Cruelty and Perfidy, scarcely paralleled in the most barbarous Ages, and totally unworthy of the Head of a civilized Nation. He has excited domestic Insurrections amongst us, and has endeavoured to bring on the Inhabitants of our Frontiers, the merciless Indian Savages, whose known Rule of Warfare, is an undistinguished Destruction, of all Ages, Sexes and Conditions."

Rumsfeld said, "The Crown is going to think you people over here in the Colonies are politically incorrect."

Jefferson said he didn't care. He read on: "We who represent the good People of these Colonies, solemnly Publish and Declare, That these United Colonies are, and of Right ought to be, FREE AND INDEPENDENT STATES; that they are absolved from all Allegiance to the British Crown, and that all political Connection between them and the State of Great-Britain, is and ought to be totally dissolved; and that as FREE AND INDEPENDENT STATES, they have full Power to levy War, conclude Peace, contract Alliances, establish Commerce, and to do all other Acts and Things which INDEPENDENT STATES may of right do. And for the support of this Declaration, with a firm Reliance on the Protection of divine Providence, we mutually pledge to each other our Lives, our Fortunes, and our sacred Honor."

Jefferson continued. "The king will have to connect the dots. Deliver it to old fatso in London and tell him we mean business."

"But," said Sir Duncan, "this could mean war."

Jefferson replied, "I didn't write this for my health."

Things in My Attic

ONE OF MY FAVORITE PLACES on Martha's Vineyard is the flea market, where people bring things from their attics of great value—or little value—whichever comes first.

My dream is to find a valuable painting that the owner doesn't know is priceless.

This week I went to the flea market with my hopes high. I passed up a teakettle from 1942, a Barbie doll with one arm, a torn quilt with the words "God Bless Our Home," a bluefish mounted on a plaque that said, "Caught by Gerry Hawke in 1971," a pair of used sneakers, the flat back tire of a bicycle and a copy of *Boys' Life*.

Of course there were other bargains, but my eye was still looking for a priceless painting—a Gauguin, a van Gogh, or an early Picasso (which I always considered to be the time of his best work).

I was going through a stack of old Coca-Cola posters at one of the booths when suddenly I saw an oil painting that looked familiar. It was a Leonardo da Vinci picture of angels having a picnic. I knew the only other one was in the Vatican. Obviously, it had dust on it, and when I wiped it off with my sleeve, it looked as if Leonardo had painted it yesterday.

I pretended I wasn't interested. This always works at the flea market because the people there like to haggle.

"That's a nice collection of Coca-Cola posters," I said.

"My grandson found them in the back of the attic in a trunk that Grandma kept."

"What is this ratty painting with saints all over it?"

"I don't know. It was in the attic with all my Coca-Cola posters, and I figured some sucker would go for it."

"Out of curiosity, how much are you asking for it?"

"I don't know, maybe $50."

I looked it over carefully. "I don't know. It's not even signed."

"I would charge a hundred if it was signed," he said.

"I'll give you thirty-five," I said.

"Make it forty-five and I'll throw in a poster of the Three Stooges."

He was getting desperate. I said, "Forty-five and also a poster of Marilyn Monroe with her skirt flying up over the subway vent."

He said, "That's my best poster."

I started to walk away. He said, "Wait, I'm reconsidering. If you want that lousy painting it's yours for $42.50."

I had him wrap it up for me. Once I locked in the deal for the Leonardo I started wandering around the flea market.

I bought a television set that was made in 1959, a twenty-four-piece set of dinnerware that had only four plates left, a silver flask with "Vancouver 1990" engraved on it and a pillow that said, "Love Me, Love My Dog." And to top it off, I had my blood pressure taken by an American Red Cross volunteer.

It was one of the most successful trips to the flea market I ever had. I couldn't wait to get to New York and show Sotheby's what I had bought.

Another Icon

ANOTHER AMERICAN ICON has landed on its keister. The banks are accused of being in on the Enron swindle. They made it possible for the company to fix its books so that loans could be listed as profits and profits could be listed as loans.

I didn't understand it when, by luck, I went into my bank and asked for a loan of $4,000 to help me buy a used Honda.

The banker replied, "We don't make loans. We arrange for people to use the money we give them so nobody can make heads or tails of it."

"I don't care what you call it as long as I get my loan," I replied.

"Now the first thing you must do is create a dummy corporation in the Cayman Islands."

"What for?"

"So people will think your Honda is there, when in fact it will be in your garage. Now you list your car in the books as an asset."

"That makes sense. I'll call the company Bad Apple."

"Then you borrow $4,000 from the bank across the street."

"I get it. I use that loan to pay you back, you clear your books, and I owe the bank across the street instead."

"Because you paid us back so quickly, your credit rating will soar. You can then go to another bank across town and borrow $10,000. You pay off the $4,000 of the previous loan and still have $6,000 left for gas and oil."

"How much can I borrow now?"

"The banks will come to you, and since you're an offshore company, they will tailor a loan for you of $100,000."

"But I only want $4,000 for my Honda."

"You have to think big. Do you know what you can do with $100,000?"

"I could buy a Mercedes-Benz."

"That would make sense, particularly since you must now move your money from the Cayman Islands to Bermuda to confuse the IRS."

"Can I quit while I'm ahead?"

"Not really," he said. "You have now reached the point where the banks are more worried about you than you are about them. They will wine and dine you and send your wife flowers."

"My wife would like that because she is against my buying a used Honda."

"The bankers are eager to throw money at you. You can buy futures in soybeans and pork bellies, sell natural gas that you don't own, and make Bad Apple one of the largest dummy corporations in the business."

"But at some time they are going to call in all my loans and I could lose my Honda."

"Not if you declare bankruptcy."

"Isn't that tacky?"

"No. Everybody's doing it."

"What do I do now?"

"Just sign this agreement. If you don't make your payment in 30 days, then we will take back the Honda."

Ashes to Ashes

I HAVE DECIDED TO DO IT. I am going to be cremated and then have my ashes dropped over every cocktail party on Martha's Vineyard. It's the only way I can make all the parties held here in the summer.

I want Cape Air, the friendly nine-seat airline, to fly me.

I imagine it this way. The plane takes off from Martha's Vineyard Airport, and Mike Wallace is in charge of dropping the ashes. As per my instructions, I want some of me to be dropped over Rose Styron's lawn. She gave so many wonderful parties when I was alive. As I fly over, Walter Cronkite says to David McCullough, "Are those Art Buchwald's ashes?"

"It's hard to say. There are so many ashes dropping on Rose's these days because she gives the most parties. It could be anybody's."

The Cape Air plane heads for Edgartown and Carol Biondi's house. All her guests look up, and once again Mike lets the ashes float down.

"Who is it?" someone asks Carol.

She replies, "Art Buchwald. He said he was coming if it killed him."

Everyone raises a glass.

The pilot turns his plane toward Rollnick's house. An Air Force jet buzzes the Cape Air plane. Mike says: "Bill and Hillary Clinton must be there. We'll drop some ashes as long as it's not a fundraiser. Buchwald never went to political fundraisers on the island." Mike drops a handful of ashes just in case it's a social gathering.

Then the pilot heads toward Chilmark and Kate Whitney's house. He asks Mike if he still has enough ashes. Mike replies, "I still have half an urn."

The party is in full swing and Kate is not only serving drinks but also lobster and fresh corn. Once again the crowd looks up to the sky.

"Who is it?" the guests ask the owner of a sailboat who is scanning the sky with binoculars.

He replies, "I'm almost sure it's Buchwald."

"It can't be. He has maintained for years he would never come to Chilmark because you always need a map."

"He must have changed his mind. After all, this is his last hurrah."

Mike says to the pilot, "I still have a quarter-tank of ashes in the urn. Take me over to Menemsha. Vernon and Ann Jordan are throwing a birthday party."

The urn is almost empty and the plane has just enough ashes left to make it back to the airport.

Mike is pleased with the evening, but waiting for his plane when they land is a Coast Guard officer who says Mike can't drop ashes without a permit.

Mike just smiles and says, "I'm sorry, and if Buchwald were here he would be sorry, too."

I Spy–You Spy

THE GOVERNMENT'S HOMELAND SECURITY plan is going along nicely, thank you.

One program Attorney General Ashcroft is enamored of is the swearing in of private citizens as "tipsters" to spy on anyone who may look suspicious.

For starters, he would ask truck drivers, taxi drivers, deliverymen and cell phone owners to report anyone they see who might be acting strangely on the highway or in the city.

Like most Americans, I thought this was a dandy idea until a psychiatrist told me: "What a wonderful opportunity for paranoids to come out of the closet. The Justice Department is going to have to figure out who is a vigilante and who is just plain sick."

"I'm sure Ashcroft's people will figure it out," I said.

The psychiatrist wasn't that sure. "Suppose the tipster is keeping his eye on the laundry hanging on his neighbor's clothesline. The shirts, undershorts and socks could be hung out in such a way that someone could read it as a code to Osama bin Laden."

That gave me something to think about.

He then said: "Now suppose there is a tipster driving along the highway. The car that just cut him off could be someone looking very suspicious. The driver gives the tipster the finger. This could either be a terrorist act or a typical example of road rage. To make sure, the highway patrol sends a helicopter to the scene and other patrol cars block off all the exits."

"Why would someone want to be a tipster?" I asked.

"For power," he replied. "If the word gets out, everyone will be scared of him. I'm not saying a tipster will catch anybody. But having these vigilantes will change everyone's way of life."

"Will tipsters be armed?"

"They are asking to be, and I'm sure they will get permission. The argument is you never know where a terrorist is going to strike next."

"So the tipsters will be part of the homeland security system?"

"They could be the heart of it. A UPS truck driver could do more for his country than a hundred lie detectors at the FBI."

"The tipster system worked well under the Nazis and the Fascists," I pointed out. "If they hadn't had tipsters, Mussolini could never have gotten the trains to run on time."

"There may be some resistance from those who can't make the cut. After all, the tipsters are the elite home-front soldiers. Americans hate to be spied on, especially by people who owe their loyalty to a higher being—in this case Attorney General Ashcroft."

Between Iraq and a Hard Place

TO INVADE OR NOT TO INVADE. That is the question. The debate is going on all over the country in earnest. Here is how it's shaping up.

Hawks: We must invade Iraq and kick Saddam's butt in.

Doves: We can't kick Saddam's butt without the approval of Congress.

Hawks: Who needs Congress? The president may kick anyone's butt he wants to.

Doves: What about Saudi Arabia? If we attack Saddam, they will cut off their oil and we'll run out in two months and have to siphon gas out of other people's cars in the mall parking lot.

Hawks: Once our ground troops knock off the Evil Power, the Saudis will have to sell us oil. The royal family has no choice.

Doves: Bush is just using the war to win the election in November.

Hawks: He is commander-in-chief. He doesn't have to stoop to political tricks to start a war.

Doves: What about television? CNN will cover it and America will witness their sons live and in color fighting in Iraqi foxholes.

Hawks: They assured us they would never show any casualties during a battle.

Doves: What about our Air Force?

Hawks: They will carpet-bomb Iraq from one end to the other, as they did in Afghanistan. And they will continue until Saddam cries "Uncle."

Doves: I thought you were going to kill him?

Hawks: He could be in a cave where no one can find him.

Doves: If we invade, it is going to cost billions and billions of dollars—and at least 250,000 troops, and the National Guard and occupying force that will have to remain there for 20 years.

Hawks: That is why we are hated all over the world.

Doves: Suppose Saddam agrees to UN inspections. Do we still invade?

Hawks: That's up to the president. He still thinks his father should have done the dirty work during Desert Storm.

Doves: Why doesn't he say so?

Hawks: He can't because he plays golf with his father.

Doves: Do you think the president will pay any attention to this debate?

Hawks: He has to if he has any chance of winning back the Senate.

Doves: I pray Saddam sees reason.

Hawks: I hope so. Because otherwise we are going to have to gas him before he gasses us.

Doves: Does the White House feel Hawkish?

Hawks: They do except for a mole who is leaking all our Iraqi plans to the *New York Times*.

Will the Real Saddam Stand Up?

IT IS NOT AS EASY to knock off Saddam Hussein as the people in Washington may want you to think.

I met Oliver Baxter III, who works for the CIA, at the bus stop outside Langley. "What's going on inside?" I inquired.

He replied, "Are you cleared for top security?"

"I wouldn't be standing waiting for a bus if I wasn't," I said. "What's going on?"

"Well, we have just discovered that there is more than one Saddam Hussein. He has lots of doubles. We are still not sure which is the real one, because everyone in Hussein's government looks alike. At least we've narrowed it down."

"What do you know so far?" I asked.

"Well, one of the Saddams has a mistress named Samira Shahbandar, and Saddam sleeps in a different place every night."

"Because of security?"

"No, because he doesn't want Mrs. Hussein to find out about her."

"What is Mrs. Hussein like?" I asked.

"She is high-maintenance. She has dyed-blond hair, wears Western clothes, and she is terribly jealous. Saddam is her first cousin. She is known in Iraq as Sajida Khayrallah. We now know they have had a stormy marriage for 32 years."

He continued, "One of the Saddams is a big spender. Sajida doesn't know it, but every time he buys a piece of jewelry for his wife, he also buys one for his mistress."

"Why don't you think he's the real one?"

"Because if he was, Sajida would kill him."

"What about the Saddam who is always on TV shooting off his rifle into the air?"

"Have you noticed he never shoots down a pigeon?"

"That could be a smoking gun," I said. "What about the Saddam we see pictured at a cabinet meeting?"

"Have you noticed the cabinet treats him with no respect?"

"The real Saddam could be the one that shows up at anti-American demonstrations and burns the American flag," I suggested.

"It would be very dangerous for the real one to show up because we might take a potshot at him."

"The plot thickens," I said.

"The one we are taking a careful look at is the 'Saddam in the Bunker' theory. We know Hussein was a big fan of Hitler's, and Saddam knows he could end up the way Adolf did."

"Including hanging out with his mistress?" I asked.

"Possibly. We know Mrs. Hussein. She would never live in a bunker."

"Hussein has a son named Uday who is a terrible man. Does he have a double, too?"

"Yes, but we don't know if the real Uday is a drunk driver or chases Iraqi girls."

"He does both. Question: If there are so many Saddam impersonators and we don't know who the real one is, does that mean we have to carpet-bomb Baghdad?"

"That's probably one of Bush's major options."

Just then the bus pulled up. As we got on, the bus driver, who knew Langley very well, said, "Watch your step."

I Hate Saddam

I HAVE A CONFESSION to make. I hate Saddam Hussein. I hate him more than anyone in the world.

I hate him even more than Washington does.

It was a shock to read in *Newsweek* that Washington didn't always hate Saddam Hussein.

According to State Department reports just released, a secretary of defense, who shall remain nameless, went over to Baghdad as a special envoy in 1983 for President Reagan. His mission was to sell Hussein biological weapons so Iraq could poison the hell out of Iran, which at that time was the United States' worst enemy.

The secretary persuaded Hussein to buy 2,200 gallons of anthrax spores, which were shipped from Manassas, Va.; 5,300 gallons of deadly botulinum, which could be loaded into warheads; and hundreds of gallons of germs that could be used to make gas gangrene.

When Saddam Hussein was losing the war against Iran, the United States also supplied him with tanks, helicopters and other military equipment.

I played no part in any of this. Unlike Washington, I hated Hussein long before he got into a war with Iran. I didn't come late into the Hating Game because every time I saw him on TV, I suspected him of one day turning against us.

The other day a diplomat friend defended the secretary for not hating Saddam at that time, and even for shaking his hand in the Iraqi capital. He said, "It's one thing to hate a dictator all the time, but it's another if you're trying to help one dictator to beat another dictator."

He said, "The fact that you support one side one day and the other side the next day is what real diplomacy is all about. That was Henry Kissinger's specialty. Suppose Iran had defeated Iraq? Don't you think the Iranians would try to build weapons of mass destruction?"

I said, "But what about all the tanks, helicopters and missiles we gave Iraq? Won't they be used against us if we go to war now?"

"If they dare use that equipment, they will get a bloody nose from the secretary of defense. It's hard for him to explain to the Pentagon why he had his picture taken in 1983 with Saddam Hussein."

My diplomat friend said, "This isn't the first time the Americans have changed enemies. Stalin was our friend during World War II, and after the war he became our mortal enemy.

"After we beat Germany and Japan, we gave them all the equipment needed to make automobiles. And even now we're urging American tourists to go to Vietnam."

"So what do we do now?" I asked.

He said, "Our plan is to bomb Baghdad in a preemptive strike and force Iraq to surrender. But after the war we're not going to help them make automobiles. The United States is no longer going to be known as Mr. Nice Guy."

To Lose One's Center

ON SEPTEMBER 11, 2001, I lost my center. That is, the world as I knew it crashed in on me, as it did for everyone else in America.

Before that day, I had dreams for my children and grandchildren. I felt safe.

Anything bad that happened was in the movies. Hollywood provided me with all my thrills and fears.

After 9/11, it took me a week to deal with the shock. I knew that I wasn't watching a movie. This was the real thing.

The TV screen became my information center.

Over and over they played the hijacked planes crashing into the World Trade Center, the Pentagon and somewhere in Pennsylvania. I saw frightened people running in the streets. I heard the wild guesses on how many people were killed and how many were injured.

At that time, no one knew who the terrorists were and no one had an answer for how four airplanes could be hijacked at the same time.

I didn't know where Afghanistan was, and I had never heard of al Qaeda or the Taliban.

For the first time, Osama bin Laden came into my life as the super-villain of 9/11. He filled me with rage. The television screen showed old photos of him and kept switching back to the World Trade Center.

I was sure we would find him and kill him.

That was the Special Forces' job.

If they want war, we'll give them war. We'll bomb them in the cities and in the caves. That is what Defense Secretary Donald Rumsfeld was saying when he came on the screen.

I thought about what Attorney General John Ashcroft would do to protect us from the enemy. How many constitutional rights would he have to take away from us to guarantee our safety?

The president said we were at war.

This wasn't a movie.

First we grieved for the victims of 9/11. Then a wave of patriotism swept the country. We were told to go about our business but to remain vigilant and alert.

As the year went by, things happened. I had lost my center, but Wall Street had lost its moral compass.

We couldn't trust anybody anymore.

The major institutions that I believed in were found to be driven by greed. We no longer believe accountants, brokers, banks and what the CEOs told us.

People's pensions were wiped out. Executives were arrested. Coming on the heels of 9/11, I didn't know whom to trust anymore.

We carpet-bombed Afghanistan, but we never found bin Laden.

We won the war, but the peace is still to come.

I tried to go about my business as I had before, but it wasn't the same and never would be.

I tried to make plans for the future, but my heart wasn't in it.

I was told by the president we have to invade Iraq, but he didn't tell me how to do it.

For the first time, I knew there was somebody out there who wanted to kill me.

In the past, I thought terrorists were people far away. After 9/11, I felt they were right next door. My world was no longer what I wanted it to be. It was not a movie.

Games Children Play

THE ALLEGED SNIPERS were caught and it is now safe to go out in the streets. I paid a visit to the Folsoms to see if they were all right.

The reason I was so concerned is that Carla Folsom was hysterical during the past several weeks.

She said, "I can't understand how anybody could do what they did."

"It's hard to figure out."

Just then Jimmy, the Folsoms' twelve-year-old, came into the room. He said, "Do you want to play a video game?"

Carla said to me, "Go ahead. He's been cooped up for three weeks."

We went to the rec room.

"What do you want to play?"

"I don't care."

"How about 'Hitman 2: Silent Assassin'?"

"What else do you have?"

"Here's one. 'Splinter Cell.' You have the right to spy, steal, destroy and assassinate to protect American freedoms. If captured, your government will disavow any knowledge of your existence."

"Is that all you've got?"

Jimmy kept going through his collection. He read from a cover. "It's time for a little urban renewal. Take command of 120 fully armed, fully loaded Meganites and stop the apocalyptic Volgara invasion through our cities. It means you have to knock down buildings and crush some pedestrians. We didn't say it would be easy but, hey, nothing is."

I picked up another game and read, "Give peace a chance. The lines of good and evil have been drawn. Your weapon is a walking death machine and your mission is to destroy everything on the planet."

Carla came down to the basement. "How are you guys doing?"

I said, "We're having a problem picking the most frightening one."

"Jimmy has one of the best collections in the neighborhood."

"The violence for a twelve-year-old boy doesn't bother you?"

"It's just a video game. By the way, Jimmy has given me a list of the new ones coming out for Christmas."

Jimmy said, "I can't wait for 'Car Stealers,' 'Torture in Iraq' and 'Blowing Up Public Schools.'"

"They all sound interesting," I said. "In my day we played Elvis Presley records. Now video games seem to be the indoor sport."

Carla said, "Thank God. It got Jimmy through the sniper crisis. He couldn't sleep while the snipers were out there."

Jimmy said, "How about 'Saving the Human Race—No Matter What the Cost'?"

"Suits me," I said. "It makes you think."

Come Fly With Me

IN 2003 THE COUNTRY celebrated the 100th anniversary of Orville and Wilbur Wright's first flight. On December 17, 1903, Orville took off near Kitty Hawk, on the Outer Banks of North Carolina, and stayed in the air for 12 seconds. Then Wilbur, on the same day, flew the same plane 852 feet in 59 seconds.

What very few people know is that it didn't work out as well as everyone expected. Two weeks later they started an airline, Wright Brothers Express, which flew between Dayton and Akron, Ohio. Two weeks after that, they filed for bankruptcy.

Orville said: "We didn't expect business to be that bad. People just weren't flying as much as we expected."

Wilbur said: "We offered discount fares, frequent-flier miles and free coffee—and we still had to go into Chapter 11. The banks wouldn't give us any more money."

Orville said, "To stay afloat, we were told we had to downsize our operation."

"The only way to do this," Wilbur said, "was to fire either Orville or myself. It hasn't been an easy time for either of us. I should have stayed because I was the more experienced pilot. I flew the plane 852 feet and Orville flew it only 120 feet."

"But," said Orville, "I was the first one to fly."

To eliminate unneeded help, the bankruptcy judge said the brothers had to fire all the ground mechanics, except the one who turned the propellers to start the plane.

The Wright brothers blamed themselves for choosing to make the first commercial route between Dayton and Akron. Orville said, "No one in Dayton wanted to go to Akron, and no one in Akron wanted to go to Dayton, so we offered flights from Dayton to Cleveland."

Wilbur said, "It didn't get us out of the red, so we asked the government to bail us out. We argued that if the Feds didn't come to our rescue, there would never be commercial aviation."

Orville said, "The government turned us down on the grounds that if flying ever caught on, many airlines would go bankrupt."

Wilbur added, "When we were turned down by the Feds, Wright Brothers stock plummeted."

Orville agreed: "Wall Street stopped believing in us. The only thing we still had was our bicycle business."

Wilbur said, "That is what we were originally noted for."

In spite of all the setbacks, the Wright brothers continued running their airline with one, then two, and then three planes—all made of muslin and plywood.

They flew to Muncie, Indiana, Paducah, Kentucky, and Ann Arbor, Michigan. The name Wright Brothers Express never caught on, so they decided to change it to United Airlines because it had more sex appeal to it, at least until it went broke.

Foreign Affairs for Dummies

THERE IS SO MUCH GOING ON in the world that every time I get lost I refer to my book, *Foreign Affairs for Dummies*.

Here is what it says:

QUESTION: If a smoking gun can't be found in Iraq, where can you find one?

ANSWER: In North Korea. They announced they have a smoking gun and are proud of it.

Q: If they can't find one in Iraq, then why should we unilaterally go there?

A: Because our troops are there. They are prepared to fight in Iraq, but they are not prepared to fight in North Korea. The Bush Administration has been ready to fight in Baghdad for over a year, and if we don't topple Saddam Hussein now the U.S. will have egg on its face.

Q: How much money will it cost us to go into Iraq and find a smoking gun?

A: Probably $200 billion.

Q: So, if we don't go into North Korea we will save $200 billion?

A: That's correct. That way the president can afford to give us another tax cut.

Q: How do our allies feel about this?

A: Most of them are for us, but don't want American troops on their soil if we go to war.

Q: Is it true when the president says that oil is not part of the equation in our foreign policy?

A: Of course it is. When you're acting diplomatically, you can't let petroleum get in the way of liberating a dictatorship.

Q: Is North Korea a dictatorship?

A: Probably, but we can't do anything about it because it's too close to China, and we don't want the Chinese to get mad at us, because they are our best trading partners.

Q: A lot of countries have smoking guns now—Pakistan, India, China, North Korea, Israel, France and Great Britain, to name a few. How many countries are we going to attack after we wipe out Iraq?

A: We're not necessarily going to attack them. In a lot of cases, we'll just bomb their smoking gun factories.

Q: Can we send UN inspectors into the countries that are suspect?

A: You can't send them into France and Great Britain because you would be violating their sovereignty.

Q: How long will it take to eliminate Saddam from power?

A: Anywhere from two weeks to two years.

Q: And how long will it take for a democratic regime to take his place?

A: Anywhere from two weeks to two years.
Q: Am I going crazy?
A: It's very possible.

The Last Pill

THOMAS GREENTREE was taking antidepressant pills. Each one cost $10.

When I saw him, he was very depressed.

He said, "I have no more money for pills. I used up my health insurance, and I can no longer borrow from my relatives."

"That's tough. What are you holding in your hand?"

"It's my last pill. After I take it, it's all over for me. I've been staring at it for hours. I'm depressed if I take it, and I'm depressed if I don't."

"That's tough."

"Maybe I shouldn't have taken them in the first place, because now I've gotten used to them."

"Couldn't you take a placebo and pretend it's an antidepressant?"

"It doesn't work for me because I know it's a placebo. Anyhow, my health plan won't pay for placebos. Would you like to see the pill?"

"Of course. This is a collector's item."

He handed the tablet to me. "Be careful," he warned, "I don't want anything to happen to it."

I examined it in the light. "It's beautiful. I saw one just like it on television. The announcer said: 'It isn't for everybody. See your doctor first.'"

Greentree said, "So I went to my doctor and he told me it's only for people who can afford it. When I went yesterday and told him I had only one pill left, he said, 'Then work yourself out of the depression like a man.'"

"That's some doctor."

"I am wrestling with the decision to take it or save it until my depression gets worse."

"How serious is it now?"

"I don't want to commit suicide."

"That's good. If you ever do, you can take the pill first. I'd give you some of mine, but they have different side effects. For example, they cheer me up, but every time I take one I feel like shoplifting."

He said, "At least you have something you can count on."

I said, "Why don't you give the last pill to the Smithsonian Institution? You would still be depressed, but you would get a tax deduction."

"I don't have a job. That's one reason I'm so depressed."

"Have you ever thought of pulling yourself up by your bootstraps?"

He replied, "Everyone tells me to do that so I won't ask them for money."

I said, "People who aren't depressed always say that. It's too bad you don't have any money. If you did, you could go to Canada and buy the antidepressants at half price."

"I think I'll take the pill now. Will you stay with me until it works?"

"Of course. That's what friends are for."

Losing Your Identity

ONE OF THE THINGS people worry about these days is losing their identity. There is something frightening about someone stealing your name and using it to charge everything from bedroom sets to Lexus convertibles.

This is how it is done. You order a camera and give your credit card number to a clerk. Someone in the store steals the number and sells it to a gang of Russian thieves in Los Angeles. They, in turn, sell your name to a group of con men in Nigeria, but your identity doesn't stay in Nigeria long. It is traded to a master of forgery in Marseilles, who trades it to a gang in Buffalo.

Now your identity is in play.

The Buffalo gang works on the telephone. One of the members says he is you and orders a motorcycle, a trip to Tahiti, theater tickets to *La Boheme* and gifts adding up to thousands of dollars.

He has a post office box in Ottawa in case someone is trying to track him.

When you get your bill, you call your credit card company.

The credit card contact says, "How do we know you're you?"

You say, "It wasn't me and you can't charge me for all the things I didn't order."

The contact man says, "You are a victim of identity theft, one of the greatest crimes in plastic history. Why didn't you tell us at the beginning that someone else was using your name?"

"That is a poor excuse. I didn't know until I got my statement," you reply.

"If we issue another card, you have to promise not to tell anyone what the number is."

"How can I charge anything if I can't give anyone my number?" you ask.

"You can, but if you use it there is a good chance you could lose your identity again. But not to worry. We will be on the lookout for the person using your card."

"Well, at least I can get back the real me," you say.

"Yes and no. Someone may steal the number on your new card and pretend he is the real you."

"Suppose I get a card in the name of another person so I would have someone else's identity?"

"The people in Buffalo would soon find out about it and you would be swimming with the fishes."

"This must be happening all the time. Isn't there some way you can stop it?"

"People pretending they are other people is one of the oldest scams of the human race, but it has never been more profitable than it is right now. At least your family knows who you are."

"I'm not so sure. The joker with my card charged a mink coat to my account, and when the bill arrived home my wife wouldn't believe me that someone else bought the coat for his girlfriend."

Whose Reality Is It?

TELEVISION KEEPS GETTING BETTER and better. At one point, it was just an entertainment medium, but now it deals with all the problems of our society.

You can find a wife on TV and also a husband. You can get therapy for any difficulty—from depression to bed-wetting.

The network shows feature couples who have committed adultery and daughters who hate their mothers.

If that isn't enough, there are shows where you can get a divorce and ones that have a judge decide a legal dispute between a claimant and his landlady, or determine if someone got diddled by his car mechanic.

There are child custody shows and programs for people with bulimia.

And there are, of course, reality shows.

Where do the producers get the people who appear on their shows?

We have to assume the people want to air their troubles for their fifteen minutes of fame. Also, it's cheaper to wash their dirty linen in public.

There are talent agents who book people for these programs.

I sat in the office of Sam Starquest, one of the hottest flesh peddlers in the business.

A secretary came in and asked, "There is a lady outside who was abused by a priest and is willing to talk about it on the air. Do you want to see her?"

"No, I've already got too many people abused by priests. They're very hard to place now."

The phone rang. Sam, on his end said, "You need two women who hate each other and want to tear out each other's hair on the Jerry Springer show? I have a pair. One woman accused the other of stealing her husband. They won't be faking it. Right. I'll send them over, but have your bodyguards on call in case anything happens."

The secretary came back in, "Maury Povich is doing a show on incest. What can we offer him?"

Sam said, "Tell him we'll get back to him. I know a brother and sister who may be willing to talk about it."

I said, "You're one busy guy."

"You better believe it. I am now looking for twenty beautiful girls who want to win a guy who they think is a millionaire. They all have to be beautiful. The theme of the program is how greedy women can be."

"I like the shows where the judge sternly chews out both the plaintiff and the defendant in the courtroom," I said.

"TV is overloaded with those kinds of shows. I have a stable of judges in the waiting room."

The secretary reappeared. "There's a couple outside who want to get a divorce on the air, and they have a lady with them who committed adultery with the husband."

Sam said, "I'll call the divorce court. In the meantime, stick them in separate offices in case they lose their tempers."

"I can't think of anything they won't put on TV," I said.

Sam replied, "Not as long as it appeals to the 18-to-45-year-old age group."

The Fight for Duct Tape

I NEVER REALIZED that duct tape would play such an important role in my life.

I was in Weaver's Hardware Store in Georgetown, and apparently Mr. Weaver knew why I was there. Without saying a word, he pointed to a shelf that said DUCT TAPE.

There was only one roll left, and just as I grabbed it a lady tried to wrestle it out of my hands.

"It's mine," she said. "I need it for homeland security."

"So do I. I need four gallons of water, a flashlight, and duct tape. There is only so much duct tape to go around, and it is allotted by your value to the country, in case we are attacked."

I then asked, "What does your husband do?"

"He's a lawyer," she said.

"He's way down on the food chain. In time of war, lawyers don't count for much."

This made her angry, and she continued to fight for the tape.

Finally Mr. Weaver came over and said, "What's going on?"

I said, "I saw the duct tape first, and she's trying to grab it from me. Besides, her husband is a lawyer and I'm a newspaperman. Who gets the duct tape first?"

Weaver said: "I prefer not to get into that. I expect to get more tape in on Thursday. Can't one of you wait until then?"

"Suppose there's an attack tomorrow?" I said. "I won't have anything to cover the cracks in the doors and the windows."

A customer watching all this said, "You shouldn't panic. I remember during the Cuban missile crisis we were all told to build bomb shelters in our back yards. I put $50,000 into mine. We had Persian carpets, leather chairs, running water, a radio scanner and the complete recordings of Frank Sinatra.

"The real problem was that my wife and kids started to brag about it and pretty soon everyone in the neighborhood knew about our shelter. The people around us decided that as long as we had such a nice bunker there was no reason for them to build theirs.

"During one scare, a dozen people showed up. When I wouldn't let them in, they started banging pots and pans. I brought out my shotgun and said I was going to shoot them. Fortunately the crisis was called off.

"I tell you this story because Americans act differently when the heat is on. This time it's a duct tape shortage. The next time it could be Aunt Jemima's pancake flour."

After hearing this story, I was ashamed of myself. I said to the lady, "Do you want the tape? We're going to need lawyers after the fighting stops."

"No," she said. "We are going to need newspapermen more than lawyers to tell us what mistakes we made. Here, take the tape."

The man who told us about his bomb shelter said, "If either of you don't want the duct tape, I'll take it."

I said, "I thought you didn't believe in civil defense anymore."

He replied, "Better safe than sorry."

Mr. Weaver said, "You have to pay cash for the tape. I am not accepting any charges in case the balloon goes up."

Yelling at the TV

CROMWELL IS MY FAVORITE inventor. He is the one who came up with the idea to put people on hold for twenty minutes and then cut them off before they get to speak to their party. The airline reservation people called him a modern-day Alexander Graham Bell.

So when he called me up the other day and told me to come over, I knew I would become a part of history.

Cromwell was in the cellar working on a large TV set.

"What do you think?"

"I think it is a nice television set."

"But this one is different. You can yell back at it."

"Wow. I've never seen a TV set that you could yell at."

"People have been dreaming of something like this for years. But no one knew how to do it. I came up with the idea to have two woofers, a digital receiver and an inverted thingamajig, which you don't plug into a wall. Who do you want to yell at?"

"How about Joe Millionaire?"

Cromwell hit his clicker. "Go," he said.

I screamed: "You may be a hunk, but you are a lying, cheating impersonator. And just because you chose a girl doesn't mean you're not going to lie and cheat and break her heart! Go away! I never want to see your face on TV again."

Evan Marriott, aka Joe Millionaire, didn't know where my voice was coming from, and later on I heard that the producers fired four technicians, because they had to blame somebody.

"Not bad," Cromwell said. "But if you're going to yell at reality shows, you have to get more vitriol in your voice. Which of the talking heads have you ever wanted to yell at?"

"That's a long list. I have always wanted to yell at Bill O'Reilly and, of course, Robert Novak, Don Imus, John McLaughlin, Chris Matthews and Rush Limbaugh, for starters."

"Well, my invention makes it possible to scream at them as much as they scream at you. Have you ever wanted to yell back at politicians?"

"Of course. Doesn't everybody?"

"Have you ever tried to yell at President Bush?"

"Yes, but so that people don't think I only yell at Republican presidents, I have always wanted to talk back to President Clinton, the first Bush, Reagan and Jimmy Carter."

Henry Kissinger came on CNN with the Capital Gang.

Cromwell said: "That is a tape of the show. Do you want to practice yelling at Kissinger?"

I said, "I've been yelling at him on the TV set for twenty years. It hasn't done any good."

"Now you can yell back at him for real if he decides to bomb Cambodia again."

"Cromwell, you are going to change the viewing habits of every American. You are also making it possible for people to let the steam out so they don't have to yell at their spouses and children anymore."

"Would you like to yell at Michael Jackson?"

I told him honestly, "I wouldn't waste my breath."

The Tip of the Iceberg

PRESIDENT BUSH keeps referring to the discovery of Iraq's missiles as "the tip of the iceberg."

There are some, not many, who feel that if weapons are the tip of the iceberg, then Mr. Bush is captain of the Titanic.

Let us suppose it is so. The captain speaks. "Mr. Rumsfeld, stay on course, straight ahead."

"Aye, aye, sir."

Mr. Ashcroft, in the crow's-nest, rings his bell and says, "Hard rudder right. Iceberg straight ahead."

The captain says, "Full speed astern!"

A passenger and large donor to the captain's steering campaign asks, "What have we struck?"

"An iceberg, but don't worry. My father ran into them in these waters all the time. Alert damage control. If there is an inquiry, we will testify we only saw the tip of the iceberg."

"Aye, aye, sir," Mr. Rumsfeld says. "I tried to steer around it, but it was too late."

The captain says, "Close all the watertight doors and don't let the passengers know that anything is wrong."

Chunks of ice are flying all over the deck.

The captain orders Mr. Powell to go below to see how much damage there is. He reports the ship is taking on water, but the damage can be repaired.

Quartermaster George Tenet reports to the bridge that his crew will go along with the captain's tip-of-the-iceberg story, but they are still worried there could be a large gash in the hull.

Mr. Rumsfeld gets on the loudspeaker and says, "Attention, passengers, we are prepared to run into any iceberg any time, anywhere, before it runs into us."

Mr. Ashcroft says, "I have a thousand people in the brig. What should I do with them?"

The captain says, "Keep them there. They may have information on icebergs that we don't have. Mr. Powell, are there any foreign ships in the area?"

Mr. Powell responds, "A French freighter, a German tanker, a Russian tugboat and a Chinese junk, but none of them will acknowledge our SOS. The only one responding is a British destroyer."

The captain says, "Keep trying. Maybe the Bulgarian navy will answer our call."

Mr. Rumsfeld, how are we fixed for lifeboats?"

"We have the most modern lifeboats in the world, as well as the most powerful flares. I have assured the passengers that if we don't destroy the iceberg now, we will have to destroy it later."

The captain asks, "Where is Mr. Cheney?"

"We don't know, sir. He is hiding on the boat somewhere, but he has been ordered not to go near the bridge in case something happens to you."

The captain says, "How much water are we taking in now?"

"So far the only complaints I've gotten are from the first-class passengers, who hope to get a rebate in case the ship goes down."

The captain says, "Lower the lifeboats."

"Yes, sir."

His order could not come at a better time. The orchestra starts playing "Nearer My God to Thee."

The War Over Abstinence

LONG BEFORE IRAQ, there was AIDS. President Bush declared war on AIDS, but now it's on the back burner. Long after Iraq is gone, AIDS will still be with us.

In the past, Bush has said that his government would not finance contraceptives for any foreign country. Federal money could not be spent for anything that would contribute to family planning or birth control.

The president was backing up the conservatives and the Christian right, who don't want their tax money used to encourage sex of any kind.

The main solution the right has for avoiding pregnancy is abstinence. And "Just Say No" is the only way to avoid getting AIDS, according to them.

Everyone knows that I have a reputation for abstinence, and all the women I know think the same way. When I asked them why, they said, "Our president is for abstinence and so is 84 percent of the Bush White House. That's up from 56 percent under Clinton."

When I asked all my lady friends why they are against sex, they replied, "Get your hands off me."

I talked to someone at the White House after Bush's announcement.

"Is the president still against issuing condoms to the world?"

"He still believes people should control their sex drives. That's the Christian way."

"But in some African countries, making love is the only indoor sport they have. If we are going to give them American movies, why can't we also supply them with contraceptives?"

"When you give them contraceptives, you are playing into the hands of Planned Parenthood, the sworn enemy of the Right."

"President Bush said in his State of the Union speech in January that he is going to give $10 billion to fight AIDS. How is he going to do it?"

"No one knows. He wants to fight HIV, but he doesn't want people to think he encourages promiscuity."

"The president is tough on the World Health Organization when it comes to family planning and condom use for AIDS prevention. U.S. delegates at an international conference in Bangkok even requested the deletion of a recommendation for 'consistent condom use' to combat HIV and sexually transmitted diseases.

"Why is the conservative Right so dead set against condoms?"

"Because it's a religion with them. Using any contraceptive to prevent babies is a sin. The president is much too busy to think about contraceptives. He'll leave that to his FDA adviser, W. David Hager, who leads the antiabortion faction in the administration."

"Will the military in the Middle East be issued prophylactics to protect themselves?"

"No, they are not there to make love, they're there to make war."

Bumper Stickers

THE LATEST WAY TO PROTEST the war is by e-mail. The advantages are that you don't have to go out into the cold, you won't go hoarse yelling, and you don't have to lie on the sidewalk. When you protest the White House by e-mail, you don't have to get a permit.

E-mail can also be used for counter-protests, which the president can read out loud when he is giving a speech.

Here are some samples of protest by computer:

"Hell no, we won't go!"

"How many people do you have to kill in Iraq to save it?"

"I didn't vote for you, cowboy."

"Go back to Crawford in 2004."

Here are some pro-war e-mails:

"Right on, Mr. Bush! We didn't elect Martin Sheen president of the United States."

"Saddam Hussein should be six feet under."

"We are fighting for freedom of speech, except for the left-wing liberal traitors, who have no right to inflict their sicky views on the rest of us."

"We'll stay in Iraq until Hell freezes over."

"Right-to-Life people support Bush's promise to destroy Baghdad."

And so it goes. You can no longer have a debate without e-mail. Congressmen avoid reading their e-mail at their own peril.

Even the media get e-mails, but they don't pay any attention to them.

Besides e-mail, another form of protest is the automobile bumper sticker. Here are some of the latest ones:

MAKE WAR NOT LOVE

IT'S THE WHITE HOUSE, STUPID

MICHAEL JACKSON DOESN'T WANT TO LOSE FACE

HONK IF YOU THINK THE PRESIDENT IS DOING THE RIGHT THING

HONK IF YOU THINK THE PRESIDENT IS DOING THE WRONG THING

HONK IF YOU HAVE NO OPINION

OSAMA BIN LADEN, PLEASE CALL YOUR MOTHER

WE NEED SMART BOMBS—NOT SMART CHILDREN

DON'T PASS ME—I LEAN TOWARDS THE LEFT

MY DAUGHTER GOES TO THE AIR FORCE ACADEMY

IF YOU HAVE TO ASK HOW MUCH THE WAR IN IRAQ WILL COST . . . YOU CAN'T AFFORD IT

WILL THE REAL SADDAM HUSSEIN PLEASE STAND UP?

TURKEY IS NOT CHOPPED LIVER

HANS BLIX, DID YOU LOOK IN SADDAM'S MUD ROOM?

I'M FOR THE U.N. UNLESS IT VOTES AGAINST AMERICA

DRIVE CAREFULLY—VICE PRESIDENT CHENEY IS IN THE TRUNK OF MY CAR

MY SUV USES MORE GAS THAN YOUR SUV

EVERY TIME I PAY MY TAXES, SOMETHING IN ME DIES

I AM A RIGHT-TO-LIFE PERSON, EXCEPT WHEN I ACQUIRE
ROAD RAGE

WHY ARE YOU STARING AT MY BUMPER STICKER?

Weapons of Mass Destruction

THE WHITE HOUSE was getting nervous. It had told the American people that it was invading Iraq to destroy its weapons of mass destruction.

The Americans didn't find any, so they called in "Spike" Valley, the CIA's expert on mass destruction, to give the president and his staff an up-to-date briefing.

Everyone gathered in the war room. Valley set up his map and began.

"Gentlemen, this is a map of the world. This is the Middle East. Iraq is here, Afghanistan is here, this is China, and next to it is North Korea. The countries that have nuclear weapons and chemical weapons are in yellow on the map, except for Iraq, which appears in blazing red. The countries that support us are in pink, and the ones in green have refused to back us in Operation Iraqi Freedom. Now I'll give you a moment to let that sink in."

The defense secretary, who shall remain nameless for security reasons, said, "Will you get on with the briefing? Does Iraq have weapons of mass destruction so we can have something to show for our bombing of the major towns and blowing up scores of Iraqi citizens?"

Spike replied, "They did have weapons of mass destruction, but they don't have them anymore."

The vice president of the United States, who could not be identified because nobody knows where he is, said, "Where are they?"

"They were smuggled out of Iraq weeks ago and hidden in Syria."

The president said, "Why didn't we think of that?"

The defense secretary said, "We can still bomb the hell out of Damascus. We have tons of weapons left over from Iraq. And it's cheaper to bomb Syria than to bring all the equipment home."

Spike said, "Hold off. We can't be trigger-happy. The weapons of mass destruction were smuggled into Syria and then sent to Lebanon by express mail."

The secretary of state said, "I don't think we should destroy Lebanon, because it will cost us a fortune to rebuild it."

Spike said "It could be a waste of time. Our man in Casablanca said a piano player at Rick's told him that the weapons were still on the dock."

The president was getting agitated and said, "So what can I tell the American people?"

"Mr. President, the weapons are now on a boat going to France."

The president said, "It figures. Now we know who the smoking gun is. If the UN refuses to do what we want, knock out Paris unilaterally."

I'll Always Have Paris

A FUNNY THING HAPPENED the other day. Actually, it was not that funny. The *International Herald Tribune* in Paris canceled my column after fifty-three years.

I am permitted to write one column every fifty years about my personal problems.

The decision to drop me was made when the *New York Times,* in an unfriendly takeover, purchased the *Washington Post's* interest in the *International Herald Tribune.*

I started on the paper in 1949 as a nightclub columnist and restaurant and movie critic. One day, soon after I got the job, the managing editor asked, "Where did you get the credentials to be a food critic?"

I said, "I was a food taster in the Marine Corps."

I also had a great deal of trouble with the French language. This presented a problem when I had to review French films. I solved it by never giving a French movie a bad notice, so a French producer could never complain.

In 1952, while writing about food, wine and song, I started a column titled "Europe's Lighter Side," which was syndicated in the United States. I wrote with tongue in cheek about Aly Khan, de Gaulle, Khrushchev, Lucky Luciano and Princess Grace's wedding.

It was the golden age for American tourists in Europe and most of us had a very good time. The *International Herald Tribune* was a lifeline to Americans in 19 countries because we printed it in English.

The column that got the most attention (and is still reprinted every year) was "Explaining Thanksgiving to the French."

I once drove to Moscow in a chauffeured Chrysler limousine. I went to Hong Kong, where I danced with Suzy Wong, and I dined with Elizabeth Taylor and Richard Burton in Rome.

I know this sounds like name-dropping, but that is what I was paid to do.

I always got along with the French. I once asked a French friend, "Why do the French dislike Americans?"

He said, "The French don't like each other, so why should they like you?"

It isn't the names but Paris that has stayed with me. The boulevards, the sidewalk cafes, the croissants and coffee, the Seine in the morning and the Seine at night, the Champs Elysees, Montmartre and the Louvre—all will remain as important parts of my days on the *Trib*.

A bientôt.

Americo-Shaft Airlines

THE EXECUTIVES of the Americo-Shaft Airlines Co. were having a celebration at the Four Seasons Hotel. They were honoring Tommy Cloud, who had just negotiated contracts with the pilots, the flight attendants and the mechanics. Tommy saved the airline $1 billion by making all the unions take drastic cuts in salaries.

When Tommy walked into the room, everyone cheered.

Arnie Blackhawk, chairman of Americo-Shaft, said, "Tommy, you are a negotiating genius. No one has been able to stick it to the unions the way you did."

Tommy replied, "That is what negotiating fair contracts is all about. You tell them that if they won't give in, the airline will go bankrupt."

"What else did you do?" Arnie asked.

Tommy answered, "I cried a lot. The unions had never seen a grown man cry."

"You didn't mention anything to them about our trust funds, bonus plans or golden parachutes, which guarantee each of our executives $5 million?"

Tommy said, "It is none of their business what we on the 40th floor do."

The vice president in charge of operations said, "All the people who took the cuts do nothing but fly the planes. What do they know about money?"

Arnie said, "Our negotiations with unions will be a textbook case for every business school in America to study. They'll teach future CEOs how to screw the unions when they grow up."

Eddie Tailspin said, "How do we keep the workers from finding out we were looking after our own interest before theirs? They may not take it quietly."

The vice president for advertising said, "We'll have a campaign on television and in the newspapers. We show a pilot, a stewardess and a mechanic. They will each say, 'Welcome to Americo-Shaft Airlines. Fly with us at half the salaries we had before.'"

An executive said, "How about, 'Take a flight with us before we go belly up'?"

The advertising VP said, "That sounds too downbeat. I think we should have a message that will make people feel good about Shaft—maybe a chorus of employees singing, 'Fly Me to the Moon.'"

Another executive said, "I hope the advertising campaign won't come out of our bonuses and pension plans."

Arnie said, "It won't show up because we will keep them hidden on the books in the Cayman Islands and list it as 'goodwill.'"

"My wife wants to buy a home in Fort Lauderdale," the VP in charge of frequent flier miles said. "Can she do it now?"

"Of course. That is what our bonus plan is for," said Arnie. "But I would sell your stock before the word gets out about our executive compensation plans."

The executives picked up their cell phones and called their brokers and then their friends and relatives.

Arnie spoke again. "I am happy to announce that we owe a lot to Tommy, and I am making him Employee of the Year. He has done more for aviation than Charles Lindbergh."

They all raised their glasses of Dom Perignon and sang, "For he's a jolly good fellow."

Tommy blushed and said, "All it took was the same greed that everyone in this room has."

Freedom of Speech

THE CONSTITUTION guarantees everyone the right to freedom of speech and the government a right to keep everything you say in a database.

For example, the federal marshals at the airports have a list of protesters. It is called the "No Fly" list and has been very helpful in finding people who are against the war in Iraq. (I did not make this up.)

Obviously, the list is quite useful in tracking down opponents of President Bush.

George Mayberry, a federal marshal at Reagan National Airport said, as he made me take off my shoes, "The No Fly list is the only way we can tell who the protesters are."

"I'm not a protester," I said, as he searched my shoes with a wand. "I think President Bush is the greatest president we've ever had."

"Your name is on the list."

"That's another Buchwald," I protested. "He is a known agitator and they always mix up our names."

Mayberry said, "Stick out your arms. Have you ever used free speech to advocate overthrowing the government?"

"Never," I said. "Not even when I went to dinner in Georgetown."

"If you were a card-carrying protester, could you give us the names of other protesters?"

I said, "I don't know anybody. Ask Don Rumsfeld and Colin Powell or Richard Perle. They make me proud to be an American."

Mayberry asked, "What have you got in your pocket?"

"A photo of Vice President Cheney. I always carry it next to my heart. Can I go now so I won't miss my plane?"

"We're not finished with you yet. Stand over there with the other No Fly suspects."

I went over to the area assigned to the outspoken protesters.

Martin Sheen said, "I think Bush and his war plans are a disgrace."

Susan Sarandon said, "I have a right to say anything I want to, even if my mother doesn't agree with me."

Tim Robbins said, "I have to get back to a peace rally in San Francisco."

A man who looked like an FBI agent was videotaping all of us.

The Dixie Chicks sang, "Ain't going to go to war no more."

I felt terrible to be put in the same class with peacenik movie stars and singers.

"What about you?" Mike Farrell asked. "What are you in for?"

I replied, "I can go either way. I don't think we should bomb innocent people, but if that is what it takes to conquer another country, I say do it."

I could see looks of disappointment in the No Fly faces, so I tried to say something positive. "Of course I am for freedom of speech. On the other hand, we must have time to find weapons of mass destruction before we start charging the White House with not doing the right thing."

My remarks didn't fly. Sheen said, "Why won't they let us get on the plane?"

I said, "Because even if you are in show business you could still be a terrorist."

Sarandon cried, "I am an actress, not a terrorist."

I said, "These are difficult times. Americans have to put up with a lot. Removing your shoes and missing your plane is a small price to pay to guarantee every citizen his freedom of speech."

The Political War

WITH THE WAR OVER, the Bush administration is hard at work preparing for the battle of 2004.

The four-star general in charge is Karl Rove, an expert in

presidential election warfare. One of his aides, who works in the basement of the White House, said, "We must defeat the Axis of Democrats and Ralph Nader no matter how much it costs. We also have to win Florida."

As an embedded political correspondent, I asked, "Do you have a plan?"

The aide replied, "We are going after the minds and hearts and votes of the American people."

"That's going to cost money," I said.

"We'll get the money. After all, we are fighting for the homeland security of the Republican Party."

"Isn't it a bit early to fight for the hearts and minds of the voters?"

The aide said, "General Rove doesn't think so. The Democrats are in disarray. They don't know who their leader will be. The general wants to make sure their morale is low."

"Good thinking," I responded. "What else are you planning?"

"We plan on dropping pamphlets from private company jets in the urban areas, warning the residents that if they desert the Republican Party they will have to live with budget deficits, wasteful spending and Ted Kennedy."

"That's fearsome."

"And if the unions don't surrender, we will turn them over to the IRS, which has no mercy."

I asked, "Will Rove observe the Geneva Convention Articles of War?"

"It depends. If he is going to lose Alabama and Mississippi, the articles go out the window. Political warfare is not a pretty business."

"What about the economy?"

"We are still blaming Clinton. In a speech to the country, we will have Bush say he is fighting against Wall Street money men who have caused the market to collapse. If elected, he will promise a chicken in every pot and a tax cut in every tax shelter."

"Suppose the Democrats counterattack?"

"As of now, President Bush holds the high ground. We are taking out ads in all the newspapers that if you vote against Bush you are voting against your commander in chief."

"What about calling the person a traitor?"

"We're saving that for the TV commercials."

Spam the Greatest Generation

DURING WORLD WAR II, the Greatest Generation ate a type of canned meat called Spam. Our troops were made to eat so much of it the GIs vowed that when the war was over they would never eat another can of Spam again. And as far as I know, they didn't.

Most veterans forgot about Spam until sometime in the early '90s, when a hacker named Eddie Nerd was fooling around with his computer and discovered he could send e-mails to people whether he knew them or not. He needed a sexy name, so he called it Spam.

Soon after that, the direct-mail advertising people hired Eddie to come up with a method to send out thousands of junk e-mail messages.

What made it beautiful is that the receiver of the Spam had no way of stopping it.

I got my first Spam message the day I bought my computer.

When I turned it on, it said, "Art, Nancy has a very important message for you."

I didn't know any Nancy, but I meet a lot of people I don't know who call me by my first name.

I opened the message and it read: "Art, whatever mortgage rate you are paying now, I can do better. Just click here for more information. And have a nice day."

I was about to call Nancy when Tom, Dick and Mary sent me messages claiming they had the lowest mortgage rates.

In a week, I started to hear from everyone. I was offered an all-expense-paid trip to Florida to buy a house, 50 percent off for a package deal to Las Vegas and a free sample of Viagra.

I couldn't wait to get home every night and find out what someone was offering me.

I made the mistake one evening of clicking on "New Club Members." Nothing serious there, I thought, but the next time I turned the computer on I was locked onto a pornography Web site. Apparently when I hit "New Club Members," I was immediately connected to porn. Porn is not my bag and does nothing for me. I tried to get it off my hard drive but it was impossible.

I talked to AOL, Yahoo and Google, but they said they couldn't help me. Once Spam gets into your computer, it has a memory all its own.

Everyone has to receive junk mail, and if you don't like it, tough luck.

The worst part about Spam is that all the politicians are now using it to send their messages to the voters. Although political campaign messages are better than porn, who is to say that when your name is sold to someone running for office it can't also be sold to any other group?

Because I am busy, sometimes I don't read all my Spam.

Sometimes I'll hear from a publisher informing me that I have won a million dollars, but before I can collect I have to subscribe to one of its publications.

I guess the Spam that is the most intriguing is the kind that reads, "Find out all about your friends and relatives. We will tell you their secrets and things you never knew about them before." CLICK.

Even though I'm getting wise to queries on the screen reading, "Do you know the sender of this e-mail?" it's hard for me to say, particularly when Nancy writes, "Hi, Art."

James Bond and WMD

I AM WRITING the next James Bond movie. The opening scene is with M calling James while he is resting with Nicole Kidman in a monastery in Tibet.

M tells him to get back right away. The next scene shows Bond in M's office.

"This is important. The Prime Minister wants you to go to Iraq and find weapons of mass destruction. He told the British people Iraq had them, and that is why we joined the U.S. in a pre-emptive war against Saddam Hussein."

"Why can't the CIA do that?"

"They assured President Bush that Iraq had the weapons, but now they just can't find any. The president is a big fan of yours and Don Rumsfeld has told him if anyone can find the WMD, Bond can."

The next scene shows Bond on an Air France plane. The beautiful stewardess (Juliette Binoche) says to him, "Why do the British hate us?"

Bond says, "We don't hate you. The Americans hate you. I'll explain it to you when we get to the Baghdad Hilton, room 25."

When he gets to his hotel, a CIA agent (Harrison Ford) who works as a room clerk, meets him in the lobby. "Welcome to the land of democracy. What brings you here?"

"I'm looking for weapons of mass destruction."

"Aren't we all?"

"Our people say that the CIA people assured Bush and Blair they were here."

"That's what they wanted to hear."

"Well, Blair could lose the election if we don't find any."

The CIA agent says, "Bush doesn't have that problem. He says Saddam has them hidden somewhere, or he destroyed them, or sold them to Syria. And he'll get re-elected even if we don't find any."

Bond says, "I think I'll take a shower. If a beautiful French stewardess asks for me let her up, and send two dry martinis, a bottle of Dom Perignon, and a pound of foie gras."

"Are we supposed to charge it to MI6?" the CIA agent asks.

Bond replies, "Charge it to the CIA. You people have more money than we do."

The next scene shows Bond getting out of the shower wearing nothing but a bath towel.

There is a knock on the door. It is Juliette Binoche. She is wearing a leather jacket and leather pants from Christian Dior. The champagne arrives a few minutes later. Bond tips the waiter and as soon as he leaves he gives the stewardess a long kiss. They fall on the bed.

The next shot pans to a rumpled bed where Juliette is smoking a Gauloise cigarette. She says, "That was fantastic. Why does the coalition hate the French people?"

"The coalition doesn't hate only the French people—it hates anyone in the UN who did not support us when we went to war."

Juliette goes to her purse and takes out a pistol. "First you make love—then you die. I am really a member of the Baath Party and you are an infidel."

Bond has his hands up, "I knew you weren't an airline stewardess when I saw a picture of Saddam in the washroom. Tell me one thing. Does Iraq have weapons of mass destruction?"

"I don't know. I am only in charge of assassinations."

Juliette pours herself a glass of champagne, and while she is putting foie gras on her toast, Bond grabs her pistol. They wrestle on the floor. The CIA room clerk comes in with three agents and takes her away.

The phone rings. Bond answers it. He tells M, "I think I found the WMD. They are on the 18th hole at the Baghdad Country Club, where the U.S. army failed to look."

M says, "That's good. Now Tony Blair won't have to resign."

The Bookies

IN SPITE OF THE MEDICARE BILL, private health insurance is now a bigger gamble than ever before. The health insurance companies are betting you will not get sick. And you are betting you will.

The health insurers are like bookies. They all want their cut.

Here is a typical scene.

MAN: I would like to place a bet that I might get sick.

HEALTH INSURANCE UNDERWRITER: We will be happy to take the bet. If we lose we pay off within thirty days.

A year goes by.

MAN: I was sick and you lost our bet. I'm still waiting to get paid.

INSURANCE CLAIM ADJUSTER: Not so fast wise guy. How do we know you were sick?

MAN: I had a herniated disc and it had to be operated on. I have all the bills from the hospital to show you.

ADJUSTER: Everyone has bills from the hospital. You have to prove your operation was necessary.

MAN: You can speak to my doctor.

ADJUSTER: Doctors don't always tell the truth. If they didn't operate they wouldn't make any money.

MAN: So how do I get you to pay off?

ADJUSTER: We have a girl named Francesca in the claims department. She decides whether you have had a necessary operation or not.

MAN: Is she a doctor?

ADJUSTER: No, but she graduated from high school with a B average.

MAN: See here, mister. We made a bet and you lost and you are trying to get out of paying me.

ADJUSTER: Did you read the fine print on your policy? It says, "In case of illness, the insurance company of the first part does not have to give the party of the second part (the client) money for five years after the policy goes into effect. All premiums collected during that period go to lawyers in case the party of the second part decides to sue the party of the first part."

MAN: I couldn't read the small print because it was too small.

ADJUSTER: I can sell you a policy for people with weak eyes.

MAN: I don't think you want to pay me.

ADJUSTER: That is not true. The other day we paid off on a policy for a lady who fell down the stairs in a department store and we settled with her for one thousand dollars as long as she doesn't tell anyone about it.

MAN: I'm getting the runaround from people I trusted and put my heart and soul in. How can you do this to somebody?

ADJUSTER: We have to make a profit too. We can't let deadbeats steal money out of the mouths of the stockholders.

MAN: Do you have a policy for people who are afraid that insurance companies will defraud them?

ADJUSTER: No, because it would be too expensive for us to pay off.

The Iraqi Stock Market

IRAQ WILL NEVER get on its feet unless it has a stock market.

Geoffrey Bottomly, an expert in finance, went over to Baghdad to give the Iraqis some advice.

"In order to have a democratic society you have to have a stock market so people can invest in the future."

"Yes," said Adama Adama, "I understand that. The U.S. fought a war so we could become part of the capitalistic system. But how do we do this?"

"You have to have private companies that make goods for the global market. To do this people have to own shares. The more shares you have the richer you become."

"I read something about it in the *Wall Street Journal*," Adama said. "But aren't some of the people in America who run these companies guilty of dirty tricks?"

"No. There are a few guys on top who dip into their company's pension funds or skim money through Panama and Lichtenstein, but we don't believe Iraq will do that because you are honest and law-abiding people. At least you will be after you get a police force."

Adama said, "If anybody steals from our people we cut off his hands."

"Let me give you an example of Western capitalism. You are the president of Infidel Saddam Gas and Oil Company. Everyone wants your gas and oil, but Americans will give you the best price for it. Oil is not why we invaded your country—in spite of what the French say," Bottomly tells Adama.

"What happens if my company loses money?" Adama asks.

"Your shareholders will be furious. And in order to placate them you, as CEO, will fire half your workers and give yourself a raise."

"You mean in America you don't cut off the hand of the CEO?"

"You don't have to. The more people you lay off the more your stock will go up."

"I'm a Shiite. Should I sell shares to the Sunnis and Kurds?"

"No, to prevent tribal war you can have a Shiite stock market, a Sunni market and a Kurdish market."

Bottomly continued, "Now this is the interesting part—if your company goes belly-up the CEO resigns."

"And that is when I cut off my own hand?"

"No, instead when you resign you get a $20 million severance pay, thousands of stock options, bonuses, a house in Greenwich Connecticut and a helicopter twice the size of the Black Hawks that are flying all over Iraq."

"Who gives me all this?"

"Your board of directors who helped you bankrupt the company. It's better to be a director than an investor."

"Can we cut off the hands of the board directors?"

"No, the directors will still have jobs as consultants to advise how to get the company out of the mess they made in the first place."

"That means no one goes to jail."

Bottomly said, "The most important thing you must do when investing in the Iraq Stock Market is not pay taxes. We have shelters in the U.S. similar to the shelters in Baghdad. As soon as the Iraqi Tax Service comes sniffing around you hide in one of your shelters."

"When do I cut off someone's hand?"

"We prefer to cut interest rates instead."

Bless the World

KELSEY KEMPER VALENTINE, the twelve-year-old daughter of a friend of mine, asked me, "Why does President Bush say at the end of his speech, 'God bless America' instead of 'God bless the world'?"

It was a very interesting question and deserved an answer.

I told her, "It's because he doesn't want God to bless everyone in the world. There are a lot of people and places he doesn't want God to bless."

"Why not?"

"When the president gets mad at someone he wants God to

know about it. For example, he certainly doesn't want God to bless Osama bin Laden or Saddam Hussein, if they are still alive."

Kelsey was listening to every word.

I continued. "And he doesn't want God to bless Castro, the Taliban or Hamas in Palestine."

Kelsey asked, "How does Bush decide who God should not bless?"

I replied, "He meets with his top advisors and they brief him on who God should bless. For example, he doesn't want anyone in the UN that voted against America to be blessed. You never heard Bush say, 'God bless France' or Germany or Russia or Iran. Once the decision is made—that's it."

Kelsey looked perplexed.

"Now it's obvious the president doesn't want God to bless terrorists. He consults with the CIA and Attorney General Ashcroft. The only time he wants God to bless them is when they have had a military trial and are going to be executed."

Kelsey nodded as I continued, "This is important. When Bush says 'God bless America,' he is not talking about *all* Americans. He is only asking God to bless Republicans, conservative supporters and Vice President Cheney. He also doesn't want God to bless liberal members of the media, and naturally, the Americans who did not support him in Iraq as well as traitors who still think there are no weapons of mass destruction in Iraq."

Kelsey asked, "How does God know who the president really wants him to bless?"

"God knows Bush very well. He knows what is really in his heart. That is what makes him a great president."

"How does God have time to do everything Mr. Bush wants him to do?"

"He makes time. America is one of his favorite causes. He

always answers President Bush's calls and never puts him on hold. Bush has a red phone on his desk, and it's a special line that no one else uses."

"Doesn't he have a cell phone when he is traveling?" Kelsey asked.

"Yes, and when he is on Air Force One he is patched into heaven. The U.S. has the most modern communications of any country in the world."

I said, "Kelsey, you are very smart to ask the question. Most adults wouldn't ask. As a matter of fact, many people think the president *is* God, which of course, is not true."

"Are you going to be in trouble for saying all this?"

"No, but Jerry Falwell will be mad as hell."

I Won't Be Home for Christmas

IT IS CHRISTMAS in the year 2020. The American troops are still in Iraq. Bing Crosby is singing "White Christmas" over the loudspeaker.

Most of the soldiers have been here since Christmas 2003. They are homesick and also mad at the presidents who succeeded Dubya.

Each one promised the men that they would be home by Christmas, but not one of them said which Christmas.

Tom Brokaw the Third (no relation to Tom Brokaw the First) is now anchorman for the merged CBS, NBC and ABC Networks. He is in Baghdad to see how morale is holding up.

On his evening news program he says, "The soldiers have just been told they will have to be here for another year—until the chaos quiets down and the various religious factions stop their fighting.

"Standing next to me is Master Sergeant Jason Marks, who has been here since the war started in 2003. He is attached to Third Infantry Division.

"Sergeant, it has been a long time, hasn't it?"

"Yeh, but somebody has to get the job done."

"Are you sorry you have to be here at Christmas time?"

"Well, if I had my druthers I'd rather be home with my grand-children. But I'm a soldier I am not going to question what the people in the Pentagon want me to do.

"The Iraqis are fine people and once the U.S. Army trains them to have a police force we'll be outta here and ready to go home."

Tom asks, "How long will it be?"

"Don't know. Every time we build a police station the Baath Party blows it up."

Brokaw says, "I'm now going to talk to a PFC tank driver named 'Peanuts' Barcelona. Peanuts how do you feel about spending another year guarding the Iraqi oil wells?"

"I'm mad as hell and I'm not going to take it anymore. My girl left me in 2012 and married the guy who fixed her water heater. It hurt because I knew her when she was thirty-five years of age."

"Is guarding the oil wells a very important job?" Tom asks.

"It's a dirty job because the sand keeps blowing up and I have to clean the engines every day."

"You are not like the sergeant I interviewed who said he would stay here as long as it was necessary."

"I only enlisted for four years and they keep extending it every Christmas. Why should I be happy?"

"Thanks Peanuts. I have a civilian here, Bill Gadzuk, who is still looking for weapons of mass destruction. Mr. Gadzuk, you started looking for the weapons in 2003. Any luck so far?"

Gadzuk says, "We're getting close. We found an abandoned mobile home rusting in a garbage dump. It could have easily been used to make poison gas. We became suspicious when we saw it had a 'For Sale' sign on the windshield."

"Any thoughts about being here for Christmas?"

"No, I am a tenor in the 1st Marine Chorus and Drum Corps, and we give a concert every year for all the troops."

Brokaw finishes his broadcast, "And so it is another Christmas in Baghdad, and although it is still not all peace, it's a good start. As the president said in his State of the Union Speech, 'We'll stay here until the job is done.'"

Who Remembers Watergate?

THE FACT THAT NIXON did or did not know about the Watergate break-in didn't bother me. What bothered me was that the people in my living room didn't know what Watergate was.

I tried to pique their interest. "Watergate was one of the most important events in the this country's history," I said.

O'Reilly asked, "Was it a dam?"

"No, it was an office building," I said patiently. "Someone broke into the Watergate to steal the files of the Democratic Party."

Their eyes glazed over. O'Reilly said, "Why the big deal? People break into buildings all the time."

"But this was a political break-in. The Republicans hired the robbers to steal the files of the Democrats. When they found out who was behind it, it became the biggest scandal in the country and brought down a president of the United States."

Bubba said, "President Kennedy?"

"No dummy. President Nixon. Don't you know who Nixon was?"

"Not really. I flunked American History."

I explained, "President Nixon went on television during the scandal and said, 'I am not a crook.' Later on they proved he lied."

Bettina, in her early thirties, and a mother of two said, "What difference does it make? I was hardly born then."

"It makes a difference because we had to know what Nixon knew and when he knew it."

Alexa said, "How did we know what he knew and when he knew it?"

"Jeb Magruder, one of the president's top aides said that he heard Nixon give the green light for the break-in. Didn't you see him on PBS the other night?"

Alexa said, "No, we were watching *American Idol.*"

I continued, even though I knew I was losing ground. "Not everyone believes Magruder because it took him thirty years to say anything."

Nelson said, "I was born in 1972, so I never read anything about it."

"Now here's the kicker," I told the group. "Several experts on Watergate don't believe Magruder's story even though he became a Presbyterian minister when he got out of jail."

I could tell by their body language that they were getting bored. I said, "Has any one of you heard of Deep Throat?"

O'Reilly said, "I thought it was a porno movie."

"No. Deep Throat was a whistleblower for Woodward and Bernstein, the two reporters who were on the story. Deep Throat met with them in a parking garage at night and gave them the roadmap to Nixon's involvement."

Nelson asked, "Who was Deep Throat?"

"Nobody knows. The reporters have kept it a secret. The only secret ever kept in Washington."

People started to leave the room one by one. It dawned on me that no one under fifty remembered Watergate.

As the last person went out the door I said, "You should have been there."

Three-Letter Word

SEX. There, I know I have your attention.

The most used and abused word in the English language is SEX. Putting it on magazine covers, mentioning it in the newspaper, advertising it on television and inserting it in a movie are just a few of the places we see it every day.

The Supreme Court has mentioned it in its decisions. The military academies try not to mention it. Priests worry about it. Both homosexuals and heterosexuals practice it.

I first discovered SEX while waiting at LaGuardia Airport. I was looking at the magazine stand and I noticed almost every magazine had the word "SEX" on the cover. It wasn't just *Playboy* and *Penthouse*—every periodical from *Cosmopolitan* to *House and Garden* was using it so that I'd buy their magazine.

When I got home I turned on the television and darned if "Sex and the City" wasn't on the air.

"That does it," I said to myself. "It is time to research the word."

I assigned the job to my assistant, Cathy Crary, who usually does my research on the federal budget. She was reluctant to take on the subject, but I told her she was doing it for her country.

This is her report.

"Originally SEX had something to do with making babies, but because it was forbidden in most cultures for anything else but pro-creating, it took on a life of its own. Since people found it very pleasurable and forbidden and fun, it wasn't necessary to use it just to produce offspring.

"Soon after, the word took on a broader meaning and the advertising industry picked it up because they found whatever was forbidden in our society sold like hotcakes.

"They said a woman couldn't be sexy if she didn't use a certain shampoo and she wasn't attractive if she didn't wear a certain per-fume, and the only reason for a lady/girl to wear a bathing suit was so other people would think she was sexy.

"Different parts of the body attracted men to women, depending on how they were treated by their mothers.

"This is not to say SEX has played a part only in men's lives. Women talk about it as much as men, and possibly more."

Cathy continued her report.

"SEX constantly rears its head in divorce cases. One or the other of the aggrieved parties claims the mate had an extramarital affair or affairs.

"The reason SEX is so popular is that Homo sapiens discov-ered it was extremely pleasurable. It is even more pleasurable than finding a parking place on Main Street on shopping day.

"The first person who discovered SEX was Hugh Hefner. He was laying out a new magazine on wild birds when he accidentally inserted a pullout of a beautiful unclothed girl.

"'Watson!' he cried over the intercom. 'I think I've got it. Instead of a magazine devoted to bird watchers, let's do one on real birds.'

"Hefner did, and for the first time SEX came out of the closet."

Cathy handed in her research. She said, "This is all I could find on the subject. Will it be enough for a whole column?"

"It is more than enough. No one knows what an important role SEX plays in our culture and if we don't tell them, who will?"

Poor Rupert Murdoch

POOR RUPERT MURDOCH. He owns newspapers, TV and cable networks, movie studios and magazines. He can hire the best lawyers in the world. He is a billionaire, yet he can't even win a lawsuit against Al Franken, the satirist (aka Flaming Liberal).

Franken is coming out with a new book titled, *Lies and the Lying Liars Who Tell Them*, subtitled, *A Fair and Balanced Look at the Right*.

The cover has a photo of Bill O'Reilly (the star Fox commentator), President Bush, and Vice President Cheney.

Murdoch had his day in court and it was a bad one. Fox maintained that the words, "Fair and Balanced" are owned by them and no one else can use them.

The Fox people asked for an injunction to keep the book from being distributed with the title.

The Judge, Denny Chin, had to decide if "Fair and Balanced" was owned by Murdoch, Al Franken, or the entire English-speaking world. He also had to decide whether putting Bill O'Reilly's photo on the cover would mean that he was endorsing the book.

Murdoch's lawyers said it was a deadly serious cover and Franken was using Fox to sell his book. The judge looked at all the evidence and then declared that Fox's case was "Wholly without merit, both factually and legally."

Legal experts said this was the first time anyone found a Murdoch-filed lawsuit without merit. Mr. Franken's lawyer said the decision was a great victory for the First Amendment.

I wasn't called as a character witness. If I had been I would be on Mr. Murdoch's side. I am a die-hard conservative, far to the right of Robert Novak. I have two subscriptions to the *National Review*, one in the office and one at home.

I read every book on the *New York Times* bestseller list that attacks liberals—who are worse than traitors and terrorists.

I send money to Jerry Falwell and Pat Robertson and all the right-wing causes. I subscribe to Murdoch's *New York Post*, which I consider my paper of record.

I would have made a telling witness for Fox because of my knowledge of the English language.

Having said all this, I think Al Franken is a troublemaker. He makes fun of the things that Americans hold dear—and he wants to make money doing it. I have another reason to suspect that Franken is a liberal. It's that he uses satire to put over one of his extreme left-wing ideas.

As Fox so ably pointed out, most people don't understand satire or that when Franken puts Bill O'Reilly on his book cover he is not calling him a liar but just joshing with him. The same goes for Bush and Cheney.

The First Amendment protects satire, but as the Fox lawyer maintained brilliantly, Franken's title was ambiguous because it did not say "parody" or "satire" on the cover. How is anybody going to know?

I, of course, believe in satire. I put it in the same class as pornography. If I ever want a picture of Bill O'Reilly on the cover of one of my books, I will never use the words "fair and balanced." Those words belong to Rupert Murdoch and I'm not going to upset him. The reason is he owns a ton of newspapers and Franken doesn't own any.

If I am going to sell my column to the Murdoch newspapers, I want him to know that I am on his side.

Senior Citizens Vote Too

I AM ALWAYS HAPPY when we approach an election year and politicians start to worry about senior citizens and how they will vote.

The main reason is that I am a senior citizen and I will take any help I can get. The reason I know I am a senior citizen is that I am not a prospect for product merchandising. I have been told by advertisers and TV networks that I don't count and that they only want to suck up to the 18-to-45-year-old age group.

Every time age discrimination is brought up it winds up in the Supreme Court, which is made up of nine senior citizens. While I would be happy to have the government pay my Medicare and pharmacy bills, the legislation has not yet passed, as it has many potholes in it, mostly put there by lobbyists. The one I lose the most sleep over has to do with urging us to give some of our Medicare business to private health plans. I am frightened that the company I sign up with will go bankrupt and the officers will wind up in Brazil.

The honorable companies have to make a profit. Since more and more senior citizens will be urged to try out the private sector, the healthcare industry will raise its prices. More senior citizens will be dropped if they become an insurance risk.

The second thing I worry about is prescription drugs. They are so expensive that the senior citizen actors in the commercials can no longer afford to play with their grandchildren.

The government does not want the drug companies to go out of business, but we've reached the point that many of us have to use all our gas money to drive to Canada to buy pills.

I don't want to be a wimp, but senior citizens have to pay $140 for a prescription. To make it up to them, they only pay $5 to go to the movies.

Because senior citizens still might buy products—even if advertisers don't want them to, it has been suggested that they carry an age identification card. The card will permit them to buy a Chevy, Chrysler, or Ford, provided they are accompanied by someone from the 18-to-45-year-old age group. Anyone who sells a car to a senior citizen that has no card will be fined $5,000.

Not all senior citizens are retired. Some are still working because the company holding their pensions spent it on other things. Advertisers should pay attention because since they still have to work, these seniors might have money for Polident, electric toothbrushes, vitamins and Viagra. So even if Pepsi wants only youth to drink their products and Anheuser-Busch wants

Bud Light Beer to be consumed by singles in bars, the senior citizen's life span is getting longer and longer.

And when the next election comes up, they will be mad as hell and not take it anymore.

The Ten Commandments

LITTLE DID MOSES KNOW when he brought down the Ten Commandments from Mt. Sinai that he would cause so much trouble in Alabama. The stone sculpture bearing the Ten Commandments has been banned from the rotunda in the Alabama Supreme Court building because it violates the separation of church and state.

As everyone knows, Moses went up the mountain alone and stayed for 40 days, after which time God gave him the Ten Commandments on stone tablets. When Moses returned to the desert, he found his people had betrayed him and had acted very badly—so badly that Moses smashed the tablets. Then he demolished the Golden Calf they had constructed. He ground the calf into powder and put it in his people's drinking water.

Then he went up the mountain again and got a second set of commandments just like those banned from public display in Montgomery, Alabama.

Everything had been going great in the state until a constitutional lawyer discovered the Ten Commandments in the rotunda of the Alabama Supreme Court. He told other constitutional lawyers who agreed it violated the constitutional separation of church and state. The lawyers won a case in court to have the commandments removed to the back where no one would read them.

There was a hue and cry over it from various religious groups who demonstrated in front of courthouse. I wasn't sure whose side I should be on so I called Moses on my heavenly cell phone.

"Moses, do you know they want to remove the Ten Commandments from the rotunda in the Alabama Supreme Court?"

"It's not a sin unless they use the Ten Commandments to justify violent demonstrations. I have this trouble all the time in democracies where people keep trying to display the commandments in government buildings."

I said, "The people who say it should not be moved declare they believe in God more than the infidels who want the constitution obeyed."

"Have the people who want the Ten Commandments returned to the rotunda read them?"

"I think so. Alabama is a very religious state. I would say they are true believers in spite of the fact they have one of the lowest literacy rates in the United States."

Moses said, "I hate to get into this fray. It's not as if they want to do away with the commandments. It has more to do with where they want to place them. I am more interested in people obeying the Ten Commandments than in where they place them. The one I really want obeyed is, 'You shall not bear false witness against your neighbor.' It keeps coming up all the time in the courts."

"Where is God in all this?" I asked.

"He hasn't paid as much attention to Alabama as he did during the civil rights demonstrations. God believes you can have the Constitution and the Commandments and they don't conflict with each other as long as you don't put the stone tablets in the rotunda."

I know there are some readers who will doubt I had this conversation, but I swear I did, so help me God.

Power Anonymous

THE WEEKLY MEETING of Power Anonymous was held in Washington.

"My name is George W. and I am a recovering power addict. I guess I inherited my liking of power from my father. I first started using power heavily when I became governor of Texas. The fellows I hung out with were all power abusers. Some drank it, and others sniffed it.

"I had no choice but to use it myself because it was in my genes. I tried to kick the habit when I came to Washington, but I didn't know this was the center of power for the free world.

"I could buy all the power I wanted on any street corner. Every time I woke up I had to have a fix. Then I would go to my office and my staff said I didn't have enough of it. It wasn't long before I started having nightmares. I believed people on the Hill were out to get me.

"Some say I am still on a power trip. But if I hadn't hit bottom I wouldn't be here tonight."

"My name is Donald R. I work in the Pentagon. As a matter of fact, I am the Pentagon. Next to George W., I have the most power in America. I can send troops anywhere I want to and no one can stop me except George W., but he never understood what real military power was all about and left the decisions up to me.

"I have more power because George believes me more than he does Colin. I got my first taste of power when, as Secretary of Defense, I was flying a fighter plane over the no-fly zone in Iraq. I saw several tanks explode and realized that I had enough power to blow up anything I wanted to. Power didn't come cheap. It cost billions and billions of dollars, but I had it to spend. The fact that I'm here tonight doesn't mean I'm cured. Any day I can go back to getting high on it. There are twelve steps to Power Anonymous. I'm still on the first one. Giving it up is much tougher than you think."

"My name is Colin P. I used to be a general but in my present job nobody really listens to me. At the beginning I was hooked on power, but as time went by it was harder and harder to keep it.

"That's one of the reasons I am coming out of the closet. If you can't get real power you can't take a chance with the adulterated stuff.

"I hope to help other secretaries of state who don't realize what so-called power trips do to your health."

"My name is Condoleezza R. and I came late to power. Originally I wanted to be a pianist, but friends got me to try power and I became high on it. I hope to break the habit because power makes me look too serious—I know how important being on *Meet the Press* is. But I also know that after all the news shows your thinking becomes fuzzy and power becomes an addiction. Power Anonymous is my last resort. If I can't stop using power I will wind up in the gutter and on the *Jerry Springer Show*."

"My name is Dick C. I don't have much power except with the energy companies. The reason I am here is that I like to circulate with all you people. George W. is my role model. Once he was power mad, but he now realizes that it is not always the answer."

The meeting adjourned and everyone had doughnuts and coffee. They promised to meet the next week—unless there was another war—in which case they all might break their vows.

A Great American

YOU HEAR IT A LOT about public figures, particularly with an election coming up. Everyone running for office is described by his introducer at every political rally as a "great American."

I have never heard anyone say a person is a "good American," but every once in awhile I hear someone called a "bad American."

The "greatest American" is President Bush (all presidents, even Nixon, have been referred to as the "greatest president" when in office). But Bush's people have gone one step farther, particularly at Republican fundraising dinners, calling him the "greatest president the country has ever had." This always is followed by a standing ovation.

Who is a "great American" and who isn't?

Let's take the attorney general as a role model. If you are in favor of his Patriot Act and don't mind your private life being scrutinized and profiled, then Ashcroft will not only consider you a "great American," but he'll also throw in the word "patriot" for free. If you raise any constitutional issues as to how he is running the Justice Department, you are a suspect and have to be watched carefully.

Just because you know the words to the "Star Spangled Banner" doesn't necessarily mean you are automatically a "great American." Even football players and Britney Spears sing the national anthem before a game.

With Iraq still in chaos, the real test of a "great American" is if you support the way Bush is handling the "Peace." This means giving him all the money he needs, defending him against the anti-Bushies that are getting more numerous every day and supporting him in plans to restart the economy.

If people who are unemployed don't complain about their status, the White House will consider them "great Americans."

Even in the government, the questions of those who are and those who aren't is still up in the air. For example, the FBI believes every member of the bureau is a "great American" (except for whistleblowers and Robert Hanssen, who is doing life for selling out his country to the Soviet Union).

The CIA claims to have more great ones than the FBI, but they can't talk about it. They have undercover agents who can't even admit they are Americans.

You don't have to be born in this country to be a "great American." Arnold Schwarzenegger is one—at least his wife Maria says he is.

In days gone by it was okay to be an American, but now with the talk show hosts yelling and name calling, they can make or break your patriotism. The dean of TV and radio talk shows is Bill O'Reilly. He makes up his audience's minds for them on where they stand. Sometimes it gets personal. For example, he believes Rupert Murdoch is a "great American" because he signs O'Reilly's paycheck.

It is much easier with the chaos in Iraq to weed out the good guys from the bad ones. If you criticize anyone in the Pentagon, you are a traitor and giving aid and comfort to Saddam Hussein.

Rush Limbaugh is also an arbiter as to who is for this country and who is not. Limbaugh speaks for the people on the Right while he trashes the people on the Left.

The only one every conservative agrees is a terrible American is Al Franken. Although he has a bestselling book, the right wing says he should either leave the country or shut up.

Where do I stand? I am going to night school and taking a course in Patriotism 101. If I pass I'll let you know.

The Big Leak

I CAME BACK FROM LUNCH and asked my assistant Cathy, "Any calls from the White House?"

"No," she said.

"Nothing from any high officials in the Administration?"

"No. The only call you got was from the laundry saying your shirts are ready."

"I don't understand it," I said. "Someone is leaking all over town to reporters about the CIA but no one is leaking to me. We didn't put the White House on the Do-Not-Call list did we?"

"No, we didn't," she said.

"I know they leaked to Robert Novak. Why him and not me?"

"He has better connections with the Administration," Cathy said. "The White House knows he'll put their spin on it."

"But so will I if they just give me a chance. Someone told Novak that an Ambassador's wife worked for the CIA, and that's against the law. If they had told me I would have printed it, and like Novak, I would never reveal my source."

Cathy said, "They don't trust you."

"That is silly. If they leaked to me I would be as trustworthy as Novak. They just won't give me a chance."

The phone rang again. Cathy answered it. I heard her say, "Yes, four o'clock at 18th and L Streets."

She hung up. I asked her, "Was that a White House leak?"

"No, it was Ritz Camera. They said your pictures would be ready at 4 o'clock."

I had nothing to do so I called the CIA. When the man answered I said, "Did you know someone in the government is leaking the names of undercover agents to the press?"

"Thanks for telling us. We never know what is going on in Washington."

"I can't give you names because I would be violating my journalistic oath, but if you read the Novak column you can connect the dots."

"We will get our people on it right away, and if what you say is true, we'll turn it over to the Justice Department who will turn it over to the FBI, which by the way, we can't stand. What is your interest in all this?"

I said, "I got the same information Novak did, but I refused to print it."

"Atta boy. We're glad you are on our side."

Cathy said, "Why did you tell him all that?"

"If the White House is going to leak to their friends they are going to have to pay for it. Let's see, how should I start the column? How about, 'Sources in the Oval Office told this reporter . . .'"

Cathy said, "It's boring."

"How about, 'I have it on the highest authority that someone in the government revealed the name of an undercover CIA agent, thus endangering the lives of hundreds of her contacts overseas.'"

"That's better," Cathy said. "Do you want to reveal the agent's name?"

"I'll save that for next week."

Unnecessary Roughness

RUSH LIMBAUGH, the serial conservative and football expert, has stepped into doo-doo over remarks he made on TV about black quarterbacks. There are three answers as to why he did it: he is a racist, his radio show is racist, and he allegedly buys painkillers in batches of 4,000 pills at a time.

What can one say if one is on Rush's side?—Which I am.

I think he has been set up by liberal left-handed black quarterbacks in the National Football League. As a defender of Rush, and there are many, I say it's harder to be a football commentator than people might think. I know Rush is not a racist. He was paid by ESPN to tell it like it is, and if a black quarterback is not carrying his weight then Rush owes it to his audience to say it.

Limbaugh was picked for the job because he brought professionalism to the game. His expert opinions on "NFL Sunday Countdown" made football a more colorful sport. He was speaking for America when he discussed the color of the football players and why they play the way they do.

ESPN knew he had strong feelings about liberals, traitors, Democrats and quarterbacks—the very things people want to hear when they watch Sunday football. As the producers told him every week, "You have the numbers. You can say anything you want to as long as you sell beer."

Now the most interesting thing about all this is that Donovan McNabb, the quarterback for the Philadelphia Eagles, does advertisements for Campbell's Chicken Soup. His commercials show him going into a family's living room in his Eagle's jersey and being served broth with lots of chicken in it. McNabb is paid ten times more than a quarterback for doing the ads.

McNabb fears that by being knocked on "NFL Sunday Countdown" by Rush that his fee for future Campbell's ads will go way down. It is really up to what kind of contract he has. If the kids stop eating the soup because McNabb is not giving his all, Campbell's may stop paying him.

Of course, Rush has his detractors, as all great commentators do. One person, a Leftie, wrote after all the fuss, "I think they should have taken his political radio show off the air and let him keep his football job."

I don't know Rush Limbaugh personally, but every time I get into a taxicab I hear his voice. Taxi drivers believe everything he says—even those who don't speak English.

Now the other subject I would like to deal with is the fact that Rush allegedly bought thousands of painkillers on the black market. Is this wrong? His supporters say he had to take painkillers after what the liberals were doing to our country. Rush didn't make a big deal of it. Only his closest friends knew about it, but once the story broke in the *National Enquirer*, everyone on the Right knew it was a put-up job.

Football is going to lose one of the great ones. Maybe they will name a stadium after him—or hang up his Brooks Brothers suit in the studio locker room.

Whatever you think of Rush Limbaugh, ESPN will never see his likes again.

But Seriously Speaking

THE QUESTION NOW is not what Arnold is going to do for California, but what is he going to do to us?

If you remember, Arnold announced he was going to enter the recall battle not to Tom Brokaw, Peter Jennings or Dan Rather, but to Jay Leno on his late night show.

Once he got into the fray, the jokes began in earnest. Comedians started to imitate Schwarzenegger's accent, they made fun of his movies, and talked about pumping iron with Madonna.

I remember saying to a Kennedy, who shall remain nameless, "How long with the Arnold jokes?"

That person said, "It will blow over. How many jokes can they tell about one man?"

I said, "There is no end to how many there are. Just his *Terminator* movies alone are fodder for every late night comedy writer in the country. Besides, California loves a governor they can really make fun of. That is why Davis had no following."

I met a Davis spin-doctor who said, "Did you hear the one about Arnold on the elevator with a lady who didn't want to be pawed?"

I replied, "I don't want to hear those kinds of jokes."

"The *Los Angeles Times* said there were 15 incidents just like it. Everyone is telling those jokes all over the country."

"That isn't why he ran for governor. He even has a financial plan for the state," I said.

The Davis man said, "That's funny in itself."

I was getting annoyed with all the jokes after hearing them more than ten times. Even Bob Novak was telling Schwarzenegger stories—some without identifying who told him.

I have to confess I was at Maria Shriver and Arnold's wedding.

I did not hear one person say, "He's a wonderful boy. Someday he is going to become governor of California." Someone might have said it, but I didn't hear him.

The most interesting thing about Arnold is that he likes to make fun of himself. It is the same self-deprecating humor he is noted for in many of his movies.

A producer said, "If someone gave me a script with Arnold playing the governor of a large state I would throw him out of the office."

"Because you can't have a governor who keeps shooting people and throwing them over his head?" I asked.

"You've got it," he replied. "In the role of governor it's not the Arnold we all know and love."

Since Arnold won the recall election, the jokes, rather than slowing down, are increasing. They come from the east coast, travel to the west coast, and then are recycled back again. The Democrats have set up a Schwarzenegger website where people can exchange Arnold stories.

Whatever happens, what we must prepare for is three years of jokes, some of them people can repeat, and some they can't.

This is a great country and we thrive on celebrities that are so well-known that you don't even have to use their last names. All you have to do is say "Arnold" and someone will tell you the latest joke.

Being governor of California is a dirty business, but somebody has to do it.

Wal-Mart

....

I AM A WAL-MART SHOPPER. I go there not because the merchandise is so good but because its floors are so clean.

The other day I asked a manager. "How do you keep the store so polished?"

He said proudly, "We have the best janitors in America. You could serve your turkey dinner on our floors."

"I wouldn't want to do that. Do you have a training school for the cleaners?"

"No, most of them come from abroad and are already trained. They come from Russia, Lithuania, Poland, and Bulgaria. We run ads in the papers over there promising the American dream."

"You don't say you want them to be floor sweepers?"

"No all we say is we will pay their fares, and guarantee them a job. Our recruiters abroad make sure they are qualified. You see that fellow over there waxing the floor in the lingerie department? He is from Estonia and has never missed a day at work."

"Does that mean he doesn't get a day off?"

"Of course he doesn't or else he couldn't put in a seven-day week."

"And he doesn't complain?"

"He is an illegal alien. Who is he going to complain to?"

The manager continued, "Wal-Mart is intent on making its employees happy. That lady over there is one of our best scrubwomen. She is from China and she is highly prized by management because she doesn't speak English. Every time the U.S. Immigration authorities raid the store she hides under the quilts and they never find her. That is the type of person who works for us."

"Why do the Feds keep raiding the store looking for illegal aliens?"

"They are very spiteful people. Look, one of the country's biggest problems is that it is sending all its jobs overseas. Wal-Mart is bringing foreigners over here and no one ever thanks us."

He said, "Most customers don't know that Wal-Mart gets their cleaning people from abroad. We are thinking about having a 'Janitors Day Sale' with 50 percent off on mops, pails and wax."

"Good idea, janitors never get the credit they deserve."

"And illegal alien cleaning people get no respect. Look, Wal-Mart is renowned for its low prices. This means cutting our payroll to the bone."

"Does Wal-Mart personally hire the people who clean its stores?"

"No, we farm out the work to janitorial specialists and they contract their work to head hunters, who then round up and put the workers on a slow boat to Baltimore."

"How do you respond to the critics who say you are running a white slavery operation?"

"We say if we can hire American janitors who will work seven days a week at minimum salaries we'll do it. But Americans are spoiled and they want days off. They don't have the drive of an Estonian worker."

"Will you have trouble finding illegal aliens if Immigration keeps raiding your store?"

"Retailing is a tough business."

"I always say the only thing that counts is the bottom line. And janitors who sweep together stay together."

Talk Show

....

I WAS WATCHING a talk show on TV the other night when the subject of profiteering from the war came up. The reason it came up was because a talking head pointed out that the Halliburton company charged $2.95 a gallon to transport oil into Iraq, while the Iraqi State Oil Marketing Organization charges 95 cents to do the same thing.

The first talking head, whom I call Big Mouth, said, "What's wrong with a company making a profit during a war? That is what the capitalistic system is all about."

The second talking head, whom I call Softball said, "It's our money. If we are asking our boys to fight in Iraq we should not sock it to the taxpayer during the occupation."

Big Mouth said, "You are mixing oranges with applesauce. Halliburton's first obligation is to its stockholders. When Halliburton signed a contract to rebuild the country it was understood by the Pentagon that they would not do it on the cheap."

Softball said, "There was no competitive bidding. If there had been, another company might have been able to do it for a lot less money."

Big Mouth said, "We will never know, will we?"

"Vice President Cheney was president of Halliburton. Did he have anything to do with the contract?"

Big Mouth said, "He certainly didn't. Cheney has never made a dime on his investments. He happens to be in a blind trust and that is why no one can find him."

"Why do we have to rebuild Iraq at such a high cost?"

"If you bomb a country you have no choice but to rebuild it.

There is a saying in the military industrial complex. 'There is no such thing as a free lunch.'"

Softball said, "I think we found that out in the past. How much is it going to cost to rebuild Iraq?"

Big Mouth replied, "Including going over the budget and making a profit? Billions of dollars, but a lot of it will be coming back here in stock dividends. That is why the Halliburton deal makes so much sense. The more it charges for shipping oil, the more it can give back to its investors."

"Are all the companies making outrageous profits on rebuilding Iraq?" Softball asked.

Big Mouth said, "Not outrageous, but reasonable profits that anyone would make if they were asked to save the infrastructure."

Then an announcer said, "We now pause for a commercial. When we come back we will ask the big question: How many American companies does it take to screw in an Iraqi light bulb? And how much will they charge?"

When he returned to my TV screen, Big Mouth said, "I hate to say this, but if you don't support the idea of rebuilding Iraq, you could be considered an anti-Bushie."

"I am not anti-Bush. At the same time I am not for the U.S. getting us into a war and making money on it," Softball said.

Big Mouth replied, "But even if it costs us we are bringing democracy to the entire Middle East. What price can you put on that?"

Softball replied, "It's priceless if it's true."

"I think you should write a letter to Halliburton telling them that what is good for Halliburton is good for America."

Softball replied, "And I'll send a copy to Cheney."

A Sexual Revolution

This column is rated "R" for grownups and politicians.

PEOPLE ALL OVER THE WORLD just celebrated World AIDS Day. Well, "celebrated" is not the right word. "Observed" is more fitting. More and more people are contracting the disease, and so far the battle is being lost. Not everyone agrees as to the best way to fight it. A tiny bit of latex divides them. It is called a condom.

Some of the most powerful institutions involved are the Vatican and conservative organizations such as the National Right to Life. The church forbids the use of condoms, not only because it doesn't believe in them, but also because they prevent bringing children into the world. Their critics say, "You could be bringing children into the world that could die of AIDS."

Since more and more people are contracting HIV, many continents that the Vatican serves (Africa and South America) have the largest numbers of victims.

The reason the conservative groups are against condoms is that they associate them with homosexuality. Handing them out is a political blow to Jerry Falwell, Pat Robertson, and the American Way.

I know condoms are not a subject to bring up at breakfast while you are reading your paper, but since it is a matter of life and death, there is really no good time. Let's be frank. Condoms are used so that a male prevents a female from having a baby. The second reason is that it prevents sexual diseases from being passed on. Condoms are not one hundred percent perfect, but then what is that has anything to do with sex? One of the most popular brands of condoms is Trojans, which have been used for generations by young, middle-aged and old men.

I have the word of the manufacturer that every Trojan is electrically tested to reduce the risk of leakage. And there is an expiration date on each package so you won't use one that has lost its integrity.

You are probably wondering why my sudden interest in condoms. It has nothing to do with what the Bush administration thinks about them. I am certain no one in the White House has ever had a need for promiscuous sex—mainly because they are too busy working for the government. But that doesn't mean they are not interested in the AIDS program. The president asked for five billion dollars to fight AIDS, but then said it was too much money to go through the pipeline. It is written in the law that the US can only give out condoms as a last resort. The reason is that Bush believes that if the populations of the world find out condoms are free, they will be encouraged to engage in unwanted sexual behavior instead of just saying "No." Also, if you are giving away contraceptives at cost you could be wasting the taxpayer's money.

It dawned on me when I saw a Viagra advertisement promising men a more fruitful sex life, that the drug companies have to set aside a lot more money to promote condoms. You can't have safe and satisfying intimate relations without protection.

My preference for protection is Trojans. At one time they were the only condoms the druggist sold. Most boys carried them, even though very few boys I knew got a chance to use them. They were the equivalent of the Good Conduct Medal.

In a perfect world you would not need contraceptives, but also in a perfect world there would be no AIDS.

Hey dude, the Barbarians are at the door.

Gotcha Saddam

OUR LONG NIGHTMARE is over. The number one serial killer in the world has been captured. Here are some questions my readers are asking.

Who do we give the $25 million in reward money to?

The answer is Halliburton. You ask why Halliburton? The answer is simple. Why not Halliburton? They claim they have been losing money on their contracts in Iraq and the twenty-five million could put them in the black. It was understood in their non-bidding contract that if Saddam was ever captured they would profit by it.

One of the clues to nabbing the "Evil Dictator" was the Yellow Cab in front of the house where Saddam was hiding. What can we make of that?

Anyone who visits New York knows it is impossible to find a Yellow Cab when you want one. The empty cab aroused suspicions when it was parked there for three days. What looked suspicious was that the meter was still running. Ordinarily a taxi driver might stop for a cup of coffee or to go to the washroom. When Saddam didn't show up, soldiers found him in an eight-by-six-foot "spider hole." Other drivers were furious because he gave all cabbies a bad name.

After Saddam was captured many people asked me who his barber was.

He was the same person who cut Charlie Manson's hair. When Saddam was taken into custody he said, "I know my rights. I am entitled to one shave." They took him to a Baghdad barber where Saddam said, "I want a trim on the sideburns, take a little off the top, and give me back the moustache I used to have so people will once again know the real Hussein." Once he was finished at the barber (Halliburton paid for the haircut) he was questioned by intelligence officers, some who even spoke Arabic. The first question was, "If you were a tree, what kind of tree would you be?" A follow-up question was, "Have you slept with any little Iraqi boys?"

It was reported Saddam was very talkative when he was captured. What did he say?

He is quoted as saying, "Does this mean I won't get my pension? Can I still use my MasterCard? What is Paris Hilton really like? Is she as nice in real life a she is in the gossip columns? If I buy one set of leg irons, will I get another one free?"

Are the media to blame for Saddam's bad image?

He thinks so. He said, "They only write about the bad things I've done and not the good things. It was my idea for the U.S. to bomb Iraq so Halliburton would rebuild it. President Bush didn't help when he called me names, which made the front pages of all the newspapers." Just before his capture Hussein met with his lawyers to decide whether to sue the *National Enquirer* for libel because they reported that he was taking painkillers without a doctor's prescription.

Now that he is in the hands of the coalition forces, what kind of punishment should be meted out?

A grand jury should decide whether he has committed any crimes that would justify his arrest. If he is tried and found guilty he should be fined $25 million and be forbidden to ever be a dictator again. But he has a right to appeal the sentence to the Supreme Court. Or he can plead guilty and be sentenced to 30 days in the Baghdad County Maximum Security jail when it is built. The contract for the prison has gone to Halliburton.

Holiday Greetings

DEAR FOLKS,

This is our yearly letter to all our friends telling you what happened to the Kleinmeister family in the past year.

We had a few minor glitches, but doesn't everybody?

Little George, aged 19, is no longer on probation. He promised the judge he would not be a hacker anymore and would stop spreading viruses throughout the entire MasterCard computer system. He is now living with his probation officer, a beautiful 29-year-old blonde, and we adore her.

Agatha, our 16-year-old, was married in November. The father of her baby is a high school football star who took Agatha to the prom. They are so cute together. If you are thinking of a wedding present, the couple is listed with Planned Parenthood.

The stories you have read about our Rod being under the influence are not true. He just loves wine—good wine—but he never drinks more than two bottles if he has to drive.

Ellen, our 23-year-old, is getting a divorce from Hairy Harry after she found out he was sleeping with his female karate students. She wants the house and $1,200 a week. The divorce could get nasty if Harry accuses her of not satisfying him in the bedroom. Ellen's lawyers want to call character witnesses who would say as far as they knew it wasn't true.

Big Jim, our oldest, was suspended by the SEC for selling penny stocks for nickels. He was told he could never work in the stock market again. He moved in with us and was promised a job at Pizza Palace as soon as they start hiring again.

Did we tell you that our nephew Billy (Edith's boy) got kicked out of law school for cheating on his exam? He tattooed his cribbing notes on his arm and the student next to him told the professor.

All in all it has been a great year, even though our car was completely totaled when another car hit me as I went through a stop sign.

Now here is the best part. Blair and I went to New York for our 30th anniversary. We stayed at the Waldorf Astoria. They gave us a beautiful room on the 42nd floor with a view overlooking all of New York. We were up there changing to go see *Hairspray* when a grid in Ohio blew out every light in New York. Blair was very good about it and didn't blame me for the blackout even though my parents still live in Cleveland.

The TV was out and so was the radio so we got to talk a lot, which after awhile can be very dangerous for a married couple. After the blackout was over we made up and Blair suggested we take a cruise.

We took a beautiful boat to the Caribbean, but two days out everyone got hit with a stomach virus and we had to sail back to Miami. Besides being sick, they wouldn't give us our money back because they said heaving over the side of the boat was an act of God.

I hope next year will be as good as this year and that you have as happy a holiday as we had.

Love, the Kleinmeisters

Saving Britney's Marriage

······································

AS SOON AS I READ that Britney Spears and Jason Allen Alexander had gotten married in Las Vegas, I called up Tiffany's and asked if the couple had registered for wedding gifts.

The saleswoman checked her computer, then she said, "They were married for fifty-five hours and then the marriage was annulled. They have been asked to send back their presents."

I thought, "Where did they go wrong? They looked happy in the wedding chapel."

Then I heard that they did make a go of it. They went to a marriage counselor recommended by a blackjack dealer at Caesar's Palace.

I have the notes of that session.

MARRIAGE COUNSELOR: What seems to be the problem?

JASON: I'm tired of being known as Mr. Britney Spears

BRITNEY: I bring in the money, so why should he complain?

COUNSELOR: How's your sex life?

BRITNEY: It is okay—nothing special.

JASON: What do you mean nothing special? You said I was the greatest lover in the world."

BRITNEY: What would any bride say on her first night?

COUNSELOR: Is this why you want an annulment?

JASON: I don't want to make love with someone who fakes it.

BRITNEY: And I'm sick and tired of being asked all the time, "Did the earth move?"

COUNSELOR: Do you two really want to save your marriage?

BRITNEY: He wants me to quit my career and have babies.

JASON: What is wrong with going back to Kentwood, Louisiana and being a housewife?

COUNSELOR: You seem to be at odds on that.

BRITNEY: If you want the truth, I think Jason's too young for me. He is a child in a man's body.

JASON: I don't want a mother.

COUNSELOR: Let it all hang out.

BRITNEY: He never picks up his socks.

JASON: I always find her bras hanging in the bathroom.

COUNSELOR: Would you be willing to stop doing that?

JASON: Where else can I put my dirty socks?

BRITNEY: I have to wash my own bras because I don't like the way the hotel does it.

COUNSELOR: Have either one of you had an affair since you were married?

JASON: No. But at breakfast she accused me of having one. I said, "How could I? I was with you all night."

BRITNEY: A woman always knows.

COUNSELOR: If I can't talk you into trying to stay together for a month, then what you are saying is you both want an annulment.

BRITNEY: "Que será, será." It's on my next album.

JASON: Will our marriage make the Guinness Book of Records?

COUNSELOR: It wouldn't surprise me.

BRITNEY: Where do we get our annulment?

COUNSELOR: In the Garden of Only Kidding at the Golden Nugget Casino.

The Opera Isn't Over

YOU HEAR A LOT about the Fat Lady, particularly in regards to the obesity news that keeps appearing in the papers.

No one has interviewed the Fat Lady, but everyone waits for her to end the opera.

As luck would have it, I went back stage during a performance of *Tristan and Isolde* and knocked on her dressing room door.

"Come in," she sang, hitting all the high notes.

"I've heard so much about you," I said, "but I never thought I'd be in your presence."

There was a knock on the door and the stage manager handed her two Big Macs, a large bag of French fries and a chocolate milk shake.

"I'm starving," she said, "and in my contract it says I can eat anything I want or I won't end the opera."

I said, "You are the poster girl for fat people. Every child wants to be just like you."

She was working on her second Big Mac. "Do you think I am as beautiful as one of Rubens' girls?"

"Better than a Rubens girl," I told her. "When you sing your chest sticks out and the audience goes wild waiting for your bosom to break through when you sing your aria."

"I'm glad you said that because many people make fun of fat people."

There was a knock on the door and the stage manager handed her a large pizza. She opened the box and cut off several slices.

"Do you always eat a pizza after two Big Macs?"

"No. Once in a while I have a bucket of Popeye's fried chicken."

She practiced, "Do-re-me-fa-so-la-ti-do." Then she said, "I have to sing perfectly if I want a standing ovation."

"You have given fat ladies a raison d'être."

"Not only that," she replied, "I've given them an excuse to eat anything they want."

"That means you wouldn't ever go on the Atkins diet."

"If I did I would lose my role in the opera."

There was a knock on the door and a voice said, "Ten minutes."

The Fat Lady put on her corset and then gargled. She took a giant Hershey bar out of her makeup table. "You want some?" she asked.

"No thanks. Do you end every opera in the country?"

"No, my twin sister Annabelle and I share the assignments. She weighs as much as I do, and in costume no one can tell the difference."

"I have heard it said that sporting events are not over until the Fat Lady sings."

"You are talking about my sister Mary Jo. She attends all sporting events and they are not over until she sings. She will be at the Super Bowl and when time runs out you will hear her voice. I'm very proud of her."

There was another knock on the door, "Three minutes."

She said, "I think I have time for a Häagen-Dazs ice cream bar." She then asked, "How do I look?"

"You look like a star. A fat star—but a star."

Knock on the door, "Two minutes."

I told her, "Break a leg."

"Come back after the opera is over and we will go to a pancake house."

Suppose They Were Wrong

THE PEOPLE IN CHARGE of justifying our war with Iraq (read the president, Colin Powell, Donald Rumsfeld, and Condoleezza Rice) claim they had good reason to believe that Iraq had weapons of mass destruction. They keep citing the CIA as their source.

"Suppose they were wrong," Klondike said.

"The CIA is never wrong," I replied. "They are this country's eyes and ears, and if they say so, then it is so. Their role is to get the information, analyze it and then send it to the White House in neatly spiral-bound books marked 'Top Secret—For Your Eyes Only.'"

Klondike said, "The big question is who analyzes it before it leaves Langley?"

"It never leaves Langley until the Director reads it and puts his name on it," I said.

Klondike, who is one of those conspiracy nuts, said, "They had ten years to find out if Saddam had WMD. What were our CIA people in Iraq doing all that time?"

"Hanging out," I said. "They didn't actually see any weapons of mass destruction, but every rug dealer on the CIA payroll swore that they had a cousin who saw them."

Klondike said, "Is it possible the CIA only reported what the administration wanted to hear?"

"They would never do that. They take an oath that they only report the facts and nothing but the facts, so help them Allah."

Klondike asked, "If the CIA is so certain there are now weapons of mass destruction, why haven't they found any?"

"Colin Powell and Condoleezza Rice insist they are still there."

"Has it ever occurred to you that they might know something you don't know?"

I said, "If they know something I don't know why don't they tell me?"

"They have to keep secrets because if the people who are hiding the WMD think we know what they know it will be harder for Don Rumsfeld to find them."

"The way you talk," I said, "you are either anti-Bush or a traitor or both."

Klondike said, "I am just an American who believes our leaders have gone astray and we are paying the price for it. I believe the problem is not what the administration does, but what it says it's doing."

"Klondike, I can't help you if you are not a believer. Somewhere outside of Baghdad there is a nuclear bomb with your name on it."

He said, "Speaking of nuclear bombs, why did the CIA report that Iraq bought uranium from Niger when it wasn't true?"

"Cheney said it was true. When Ambassador Joseph Wilson said it wasn't true someone leaked the name of his wife, who was in the CIA. That someone leaked it to Robert Novak. I know Robert Novak, and the only reason he printed her name is that Bob is a patriot first and a newspaper columnist second."

"Why is the CIA so determined to find out who leaked the information to Novak?" Klondike wanted to know.

"It takes the weapons of mass destruction issue off the front pages and forces Attorney General Ashcroft to bow out because he may know who the leaker is."

Klondike said, "Nothing is simple in Washington if you question it. What about former Secretary of the Treasury Paul O'Neill?"

"What about him?"

"He said Bush wanted to attack Iraq even before the CIA told him it was a good idea."

"We only have O'Neill's word on this," I said. "Wait until Dick Cheney writes his book, then we will really know what took place in those cabinet meetings."

Klondike asked, "Do you think the public is confused by all this?"

"Not if they believe that the CIA never makes mistakes."

War of the Steroids

EVERYONE TOOK what he or she wanted from the president's State of the Union speech. My ears pricked up when he talked about steroids. He was obviously against them. How, I wondered, did steroids get into the president's speech?

Here is one version. The president was reading the sports pages about all the drugs that athletes are using. It suddenly dawned on him that there was no mention of steroids in his State of the Union speech. He called in his writers and said, " Why is there no mention of steroids in my speech?"

"We were saving it for the opening of the summer Olympics."

"I want to mention it now before the Democrats do."

A speechwriter said, "If we talk about steroids people will forget about the unemployment figures."

Another writer said, "Why don't you say, 'When I was governor of Texas I was a 140-pound weakling. Everyone was pushing me around. Then I started using steroids and lifting weights. In no time the muscles in my arms expanded and I weighed 200 pounds.'"

Bush said, "I don't want anyone to think steroids had anything to do with my winning the election in Florida."

The writer said, "And then, Mr. President, you can say, 'If the Democrats push me around I'll give them a poke in the nose they will never forget.' That should please the conservatives."

"The question is," the president said, "am I for steroids or against them?"

The first writer said, "We better call in Karl Rove."

Rove came in and Bush said, "Karl, where do I stand on steroids?"

Rove looked in his black election book and then said, "The pollsters don't consider steroids a big election issue. People say they are more interested in jobs than in athletes who take body-building drugs."

The president said, "Then should I come out against them in my State of the Union speech?"

Rove said, "It can't hurt. You may lose the baseball player vote, but you will keep the golfer vote."

The president asked, "Who should sit next to Mrs. Bush in the balcony?"

A writer said, "Rush Limbaugh. And on her other side a professional football player who has been rehabilitated at Betty Ford's."

Karl Rove said, "Keep it simple. Appeal to children who watch sporting events on TV and don't see anything wrong with a hockey player improving his game."

"Do we have a letter I can read from an eleven-year-old child who thanks me for my message about steroids?" Bush asked.

"I am sure there is one," the writer replied. "I know we have hundreds about Pete Rose getting in the Hall of Fame."

"Should we also warn the kids against gambling?" the other writer asked.

Rove replied, "We better not. Bill Bennett may think we are talking about him."

The president said, "To make sure people know I mean business I want everyone in my administration to take a drug test. I'll take it out of our Homeland Security budget."

Rove said, "You come up with all the good ideas, Mr. President."

A writer agreed, "It will bring the Republicans to their feet."

Four Letter Words and More

NINETY MILLION PEOPLE watched the *Super Bowl*, and every one of them claimed he or she saw Janet Jackson's dance number.

Of the 90 million, 89,995,000 were outraged and demanded to know what the FCC was going to do about it.

But it wasn't really Janet Jackson who started the ball rolling. It really started when the singer Bono said "F— brilliant!" on the *2003 Golden Globe Awards Show*. (Unlike television this is a family newspaper so I cannot use the real word in this column.)

Since the Golden Globes is a NBC network show, the FCC held a hearing, and against Chairman Michael Powell's wishes, said NBC could not be fined because Bono used the "F" word as an adjective, not as a noun or a verb.

Now here is the problem. The networks may not use cuss words on the air, but if you click to cable you can hear any forbidden phrase in the English language.

Larry David's *Curb Your Enthusiasm* is chock full indecent

phrases. *The Sopranos* on HBO tells you what life in New Jersey is really like. George Carlin and Dennis Miller need the expletives to get their laughs.

What has happened lately is women are using the F-word more than ever. Just watch *Sex and the City*.

On some shows the obscene words have become a mantra. Although network TV and radio are monitored carefully by the FCC, cable gets a free ride because people pay for it. The First Amendment protects what you hear on cable TV.

Cable TV has been a boon for writers because the F-word has made it easier for them to write a script. Every time one of the characters has nothing to say the writer gives them a cuss word.

The FCC ruled, with Powell in the minority, that it is all right to use the F-word as long as it doesn't describe a sexual act.

Some people ask, "Why do the cable TV shows allow this kind of language on the air?"

The answer is they are appealing to the 18-to-35-year-old age group—the people the advertisers will kill for.

The fact that children and senior citizens are exposed to the curse words is unavoidable.

The cable stations maintain the kids don't learn the naughty language from their programs. A spokesman said, "They learn it from each other. Even in my house my daughter uses the F-word. I asked her where she learned it and she said from her sixteen-year-old brother in the basement. A study shows that underprivileged children who come from homes without cable TV use profanity as much as those whose parents are cable subscribers. The law is very clear about obscenity. You know it when you hear it."

Several organizations are in opposition to the expletives on TV and are fighting it. They have a lobbying group in Washington. The problem is most politicians use bad language, particularly during an election year. So where does that leave the rest of us who use it only when angry or frustrated?

I use it sparingly. For example if another car tries to pass me on the road I yell out the window, "*&^%$#c!"

Or if I get a junk telephone call I might retort, "@#$%^ you!"

I have to be honest. I used it while watching the State of the Union speech. But it was no big deal. This is still a free country.

When Hollywood is making a war movie every soldier in the picture has to precede a sentence by using a curse word.

That's all I have to say on the subject. Remember, if you use the F-word, only use it as an adjective and never a noun.

Duck Hunting with Scalia

THE THING SUPREME COURT Justice Antonin Scalia and Vice President Dick Cheney have in common is they both love to shoot ducks.

There's nothing wrong with that, right? The only thing the anti-duck hunters object to is that Justice Scalia agreed to hear a case in which Cheney was a defendant.

You have to put this in perspective. The Supreme Court hearing had nothing to do with shooting fowl and Scalia refused to recuse himself (bow out) from the cases, saying one thing had nothing to do with the other.

Based on what he said, I imagined what was going on in the duck blind. Both men are knee deep in the marsh wearing camouflage suits.

Bang, bang.

"Good shot, Dick. I think you got one."

"Go ahead, Tony. They will be taking to the air any moment."

"Who put out the duck decoys?"

"The Secret Service. They have been working all night. It's part of Homeland Security."

"That is a beautiful duck call—almost like the real thing."

"That's Don Rumsfeld. He is a master duck caller. He was very flattered that I invited him instead of Colin Powell."

A few minutes later dozens of mallards settled amongst the decoys.

Bang. Bang.

"Dick, ain't this fun? Nothing makes you forget the Constitution better than holding a good shotgun in your hands. Where did you get yours?"

"From Halliburton. It was a goodbye gift. Anything going on at the court I should know about?"

"I can't talk about it, Dick, but let's say we have all our ducks in a row."

Cheney laughed. "Then could you say it's duck soup?"

Bang. Bang.

Scalia hit two more birds and said to Cheney, "I'm glad I voted for ducks to get the death penalty."

"Who are you going to give your ducks to?"

"The Supreme Court dining room chef. The members of the court are tired of pizza and will welcome duck l'orange on the menu. The key to a Supreme Court Justice's decision is through his stomach."

"Do you think the media will give you a bad time for hunting with me?"

"They wouldn't dare. We're friends, and we were friends long before your case was put on the docket. If they ask me why I haven't recused myself I'll say, 'The court never discusses why a member thinks the way he does.'"

Bang! Bang!

"Tony, I feel the same way. If I thought you had a conflict by hearing my case I would tell you so."

"I know you would, Dick. You know what? I will bring back ducks for Clarence Thomas, William Rehnquist, Anthony Kennedy, and Sandra Day O'Connor. I know she likes duck and she could be the swing vote."

Just then a dog came out of the marsh holding a duck in his mouth.

Scalia said, "What a smart retriever. Where did you find him?"

Cheney said, "He is the president's dog. He loaned me Barney for the week."

Both men heard Rumsfeld's duck call in the distance, "Onk, onk. Onk, onk."

Just Good Friends—Bah

THE CONTROVERSY OVER who should be allowed to marry and who shouldn't couldn't have come at a worse time. It reached its pinnacle the same week the Mattel Toy Company announced that after all these years Barbie and Ken are splitting up.

"Why?" asked Ethel Brooks, who has been collecting Barbie dolls since she was ten years old.

"It's a tough question," I said. "Marriages go stale and Ken was going through a midlife crisis."

"Was there another woman?"

"The gossip is that he was fooling around with Midge. Barbie got mad and started dating G.I. Joe," I replied.

"One of the things I heard," Ethel said, "is that Barbie went on the Atkins diet and was miserable."

"Could be," I said.

"I heard at the hairdresser's that Barbie took up with a young man half her age like Demi Moore did." Ethel continued, "The girls said she called him her Toy Boy."

"Women do that all the time. Bush has never mentioned anything about older women and younger men when referring to marriage."

"Barbie is not gay, is she?" Ethel wanted know.

"No. She showed up at City Hall in San Francisco to protest the ban on gay marriages. People want a constitutional amendment defining marriage as a union between a man and a woman."

Ethel said, "Half the country's marriages end up in divorce. Why don't they have a constitutional amendment for divorced people?"

I said, "Because President Bush doesn't believe in divorce. He sees the family as four people gathered around the fireplace, watching Fox television."

"Now that she has split with Ken, does she have to find a job?"

"Yes. The problem is that there are no jobs, especially for single women."

Ethel said, "Of course Barbie will keep all her clothes."

"Of course. What would Ken do with them? But they are going

to have to divvy up the rest of the stuff—the house, the Volvo, the TV set. If they are smart they will each get a lawyer."

Ethel said, "The split is going to get expensive. The only ones who profit from a couple getting a divorce are the lawyers."

"Despite all the fuss, Ken was a beach bum and then a ski bum. This attracted Barbie to him, but after a while she wanted a solid guy. This happens as time goes by. After awhile who cares what a hunk in a bathing suit looks like?"

Ethel seemed disturbed. "Do you think after the breakup they will still be good friends?"

"It's hard to remain friends with someone after living in a trunk together for so long. You know too much about each other."

"They never did get married?"

"No," I said, "but rumor has it that one night they got plastered in Las Vegas, got married and had it annulled the next day. It was kept secret because Mattel didn't want anyone to know about it."

"Thousands of little girls bought Barbie wedding gowns but never used them," Ethel said.

"People bought a lot of things that their daughters never used. How about when she pretended she was an astronaut?"

"Well, it is a whole new ball game," Ethel said.

"You can say that again. Barbie is going to use her maiden name."

Who Killed Jesus?

OKAY, I AM GOING TO SAY IT one more time. I did not kill Jesus Christ. I might not have even mentioned it except that Mel

Gibson's film, *The Passion of the Christ*, has become a happening. The picture deals with the last twelve hours of Jesus' life and is based on the Gospels.

According to the Gospels, the Jewish priests were responsible for his death, even though Christ was Jewish.

Everyone is entitled to interpret the Bible as he sees it—and even make a movie of it—but unfortunately *The Passion* has once again stirred up the old prejudices on the subject.

For centuries the word was out that the Jews had killed Jesus because they wouldn't accept him as the Son of God. All sorts of attacks have been made on them through the ages because of this. Ever since I was a boy I have had to defend the fact that I did not have anything to do with it. In the schoolyard Italian kids, Irish kids, and choirboys from Our Lady of Mercy School accused me of the crime.

Most of them were bigger than I was. The daily conversation went like this.

"Who killed Christ?"

"I don't know."

"Yes you do. You killed Christ."

"Did not."

"Did too. If you don't admit you did we will break your nose."

"Okay, I killed Christ. Now will you get off me and let me go home?"

Sometimes the confession was enough. Other times I got a bloody nose—if I was lucky.

It got no better as I grew up. I have to admit that everyone believed I was at the Crucifixion, particularly at Christmas and Easter. Those are the times when the churchgoers mentioned it and I had to defend myself against the charges.

I was always on guard because at any time someone could call me a Christ-killer.

I didn't realize how virulent the subject was until I grew up. Everywhere I went people eventually let their real feelings out.

At a dinner party the other evening someone said, "Why haven't the Jews accepted our Lord as their savior?"

I replied, "I really don't know. I can't think of a people who have suffered so much because of not accepting Him as the Messiah."

"I am going to ask you once again. Did you kill Christ?"

"I have been saying it all my life. No! I wasn't even there."

"Well, if you didn't who did?"

"It could have been anybody. Look, I thought Jesus was a great man—a man who preached love and forgiveness. His teachings have been passed down through the generations. But people have used his crucifixion as an excuse to kill other people. That isn't what Christ had in mind."

"Do you think Mel Gibson should have made his movie?"

"Why not? As long as people don't walk away from it saying I killed Christ."

"They won't. We live in modern times and we know that the Passion took place long, long ago."

"I hope you are right."

"But that doesn't mean you can join our country club."

"It's no big deal because I don't play golf."

The Good Americans

OFF SHORE JOBS—we hear it more and more. It means jobs are leaving this country because labor is so much cheaper overseas than it is in the United States. Written by a Chinese person, this column would cost only 50 cents. It scares the heck out of me.

There are now companies specializing in outsourcing American jobs.

"Marvelous Jobs Overseas Incorporated. How can I help you?"

"This is the Great American Sweatshirt Company. We want to print two million, five hundred shirts with President Bush's picture on the front and 'God Bless America' on the back. Where can I have them done?"

"Singapore makes lovely 'God Bless America' sweatshirts. You can get them for 25¢."

"We need them before the conventions."

"We'll put a rush order on them. What else?"

"The Democrats want the American flag on the back and a picture of Kerry serving in Viet Nam."

"Will do."

- - -

"Hello. This is the Patriot Sneaker Company. You know, the one who has had its factory in Rhode Island for 100 years. We decided to close it up when we found out we could get the shoes made overseas for half the price and no health insurance costs or Christmas turkeys."

"Thailand makes nifty sneakers. Most of the good American footwear is made in Bangkok. Are the people in Rhode Island going to make a stink?"

"No. They understand it's business and not something personal."

- - -

"This is the University Testing Institute. We want to have our student tests marked overseas. Would you recommend a country where we could send our multiple choice questions for scoring?"

"Burma is famous for out-sourcing college exams. Their people can do it for 13¢ per hour. They have a contract to handle all the U.S. Social Security paperwork. We can also recommend Bangladesh who does all the tests for Harvard."

— — —

"This is the Home of the Brave Canteen Company. We are bidding to supply all the canteens for the U.S. Army for four billion dollars. The rules are that only American companies can bid on the contract. We are looking for a subcontractor in a foreign country that could actually manufacture the canteens."

"This may surprise you, but Ho Chi Minh City has one of the best canteen makers in the world. The company was started by a consortium of Viet Cong businessmen. After the canteens are made they are shipped to Hong Kong where workers stamp on them, 'Made in America.' Then they are shipped to Iraq."

"How about American taxes?"

"You don't have to pay any if you set up a tax shelter in Panama."

"Thank you. We'll call you back if we get the contract."

— — —

"This is the Betsy Ross Girl Scout Chocolate Cookie Company. We recently closed our chocolate cookie factory in the United States and opened a bakery in Nigeria, which saved us five million dollars a month.

"The bad news is Congress is holding hearings on American jobs fleeing overseas. We are being called to testify. What should we say?"

"Take the Fifth and tell them that anything you say about jobs abroad will incriminate you."

"Good idea."

"As part of our service we supply a damage control team who will issue press releases saying that unemployment is part of the American Dream."

Canada, My Canada

UP UNTIL RECENTLY, Americans knew little about Canada except that the people there play hockey and occasionally blow out the lights in the northeast part of the United States.

One of the reasons there was no interest is that Canada rarely does anything to provoke us. The country was never listed by Bush in the Axis of Evil or as an enemy, like the United Nations (even though half of Canada speaks French.)

At best no one ever took Canada seriously until recently, when Canada went into the prescription drug business. It was not planned, but an accident.

A senior citizen went to Canada to visit a cousin on the tundra and take photos of moose. As he crossed the border he remembered he had forgotten his antidepressant Zoloft. A snappy Mountie on a horse directed him to a pharmacy in Winnipeg. The senior told the druggist, "I don't have a prescription," and the druggist said, "You don't need one. We are not a third-rate Central American country."

After the druggist gave him the drugs he said, "That will be half the price of what you pay for it in the United States."

"How can the drug companies sell the same drugs in Canada for half the price?"

"They don't have to pay for advertising or marketing. Also, drug companies charge whatever the market will bear. In China they are even cheaper than here. What has the senior citizens really screwed is that in your country under the Medicare rules, you still have to pay double what you do up here."

"Why?"

"Your president lied to you about what they cost and the drug lobbyists lied to him."

When the senior citizen got back home he told all his friends how cheap drugs were in Canada. They immediately started to go there. Even with the high cost of gas the drugs were still cheaper than in the United States.

American citizens with high blood pressure, arthritis and a need for antibiotics traveled to Canada. They started collecting trading cards of Canadian hockey stars. It was the golden age of Canadian-American relations.

Then Canada came up with a stellar idea. Instead of Americans going up there to buy their meds, they can now buy them on the Web—even Viagra. Any prescription drug advertised on the evening news and *American Idol* can be purchased north of the border with one click of your mouse.

A Canadian friend of mine, Norman Richler, said, "You need us more than we need you."

"You don't have to rub it in," I said. "If the American drug companies lowered their prices no one would buy anything except Kleenex from Canada."

Norman said, "Well, it would be a miracle. Drug companies

don't lower prices, they raise them. We also win the price war on generic drugs. It if wasn't for Canada, many of your people couldn't afford to take Prozac."

"Right, but instead of needling me you should thank us for what we are doing for your economy."

He said, "Will you stop thinking of Canada as a banana republic?"

"Okay, here goes." I started to sing, "O Canada."

The Blues Brothers

I TRAVELED TO ATLANTA, GEORGIA, where I appeared on a panel on depression. It was held at Skyland Trail, a home that takes care of the mentally ill, and it was co-sponsored by the Department of Psychiatry at Emory University.

I know what you are saying. "What was he doing on a panel discussing depression?"

The answer is that Mike Wallace and I came out of the closet on *Larry King Live* and confessed we both had severe depressions.

Bill Styron, the author of *Sophie's Choice*, was also on the panel. We had our depressions at about the same time and we call ourselves the "Blues Brothers." Because we went public, we became poster boys for depression. When I confessed I had had two, Styron said, "If you have one more they will put you in the 'Depression Hall of Fame.'"

Tom Johnson, former president of CNN, moderated the panel. Also on board were renowned psychiatrists Charles

Nemeroff and William McDonald. The topics discussed were all the phases of depression. (If I am depressing you, you don't have to read any farther.)

One subject was the stigma the public attaches to the disease. If you have a broken leg or an aching back, people are sympathetic and so is your health insurance company. If you have a depression, people don't want to hear about it. Even worse, the health insurance company puts you in their "lousy risk" database. Once you get in their computer no company will hire you, or promote you, and you will be the first one to lose your job.

The subject of anti-depression drugs came up. Why do the pills cost half the price in Canada that they do in the United States? The reason they cost so much in the U.S. is that the drug companies have to pay for research, advertising, door-to-door marketing, and of course, Caribbean cruises, golf country club memberships, Broadway theater tickets, and ski trips for doctors whom they hope will prescribe their medicines. The drug companies call Canada a "loss leader."

The audience laughed when one of the panelists asked if you got your pills in Canada, would you only have half a depression?

This was followed by a question to the psychiatrists: "Why do we laugh when we hear the word 'depression'?"

Dr. McDonald said, "We laugh out of fear," and Dr. Nemeroff said, "It is anxious laughter and the laughter is saying 'There but for the grace of God go I.'"

The question of the state of mental health after September 11 came up. Both doctors said that the country is not in good shape because every time someone turns on his television set and sees what is going on, his or her stress factor reaches new levels. The hourly news triggers depression in people. Anxiety is now part of our everyday life.

In many cases pills are handed out to those who either need them or think they need them because TV ads told them they need them.

The panel concluded that if you or your loved one is depressed, seek help. Don't pretend you can handle it alone.

The "Blues Brothers," having licked their depressions (for the moment), still joke about it to each other. Styron insists his depression was a 9.7 on the Richter scale and mine was only a rainy day in Disneyworld.

Our message to one and all is, "Don't do anything to hurt yourself, like commit suicide, because you might change your mind two weeks later."

Soldiers of Fortune

WHAT WE DIDN'T KNOW THEN, and what we now know, is that not only soldiers were involved in the alleged Iraq prison abuse scandals. Some of the people were civilians contracted to do the dirty work. Their job, for which they were highly paid, was to get information out of Iraqi prisoners one way or the other. One way was when the higher-ups were looking and another way was when they weren't.

The reason the CIA was so happy to use the soldiers of fortune is that they don't have to play by the rules, and if they were caught orchestrating a pornographic prison tableaux they could not be court martialed or even given a letter of reprimand.

No one knows how many contractees are working for us in

Iraq, but it's a very profitable business for contractors who supply the help. Not only do they do intelligence work, they also go on special operations. This causes some friction because the soldier in the Humvee is paid peanuts compared to the civilian riding next to him. While the G.I. in Iraq is fighting to make the world safe for democracy, the contractees are fighting for a raise.

I spoke to an ex-soldier of fortune who defended the companies who were hired to supplement the military's work. "We are serving a patriotic need and if we make a profit fighting for our country, that is what capitalism is all about."

"How did your company find you?"

"In the help-wanted ads. I saw one which said, 'Wanted—ex-military types who still enjoy gathering intelligence. Must be thoroughly knowledgeable in methods of retrieving information from reluctant suspects. This includes use of lit cigarettes, freezing water, and electrodes. Mercenaries must work long hours to break down prisoners but will be paid overtime. If suspect gives vital information, you will receive a bonus and a week's vacation at Guantanamo Bay.'"

"I can see why you signed up," I said.

"The thing that really got me is that it was tax free. I figured if I worked there for a year I could open a day-care center with my wife."

"And it paid off?"

"It sure did. I didn't spend a dime in Iraq because the CIA picked up the tab for everything, including my laundry."

"Since the news broke about the Abu Ghraib prison do people give you a bad time?"

"On the contrary. I have been on all the TV shows. The audience wants to see a live soldier of fortune. I am also writing a book, *Hitting the Soles of Their Feet.*"

"What other perks do you receive?"

"I can still go to the CIA Officer's Club and get a loan from the agency's credit union."

"Do you get a pension from the company you worked for?"

"Yes. I get $1,000 for every month I served and also stock options, which have paid off, since my business is one of the largest growth industries in the world."

I said, "If it weren't for the photos from Abu Ghraib we would never know about your work."

"We didn't take those pictures. They were very dark and grainy."

"Do you have any idea how much the civilian contract for Iraq is worth?"

"No, but we were told to get our intelligence whatever the cost."

Torture 101

THE WORD FROM THE JUSTICE DEPARTMENT is that torture is okay as long as you don't hurt anyone. John Ashcroft's people handed down a ruling to the CIA and the Pentagon that torture is justified, but only when trying to get someone to spill the beans.

Where do law students learn this?

I take you to Slam Dunk Law School, where Professor Garroting is holding a class in Torture 101.

PROFESSOR: Students, this is a very important course, especially for those seeking employment in the Justice Department. What is the definition of "torture?"

STUDENT: It is making another person say something he doesn't want to.

PROFESSOR: Good. When is it lawful?

STUDENT: When the country is at war and the president is looking the other way. Professor Garroting, does this mean you can force a prisoner to go naked?

PROFESSOR: Yes, but it is unlawful to take pictures of him and then give them to the media.

STUDENT: When deciding which torture is legal, what guidelines should we use?

PROFESSOR: The rule is, if the prisoners are held without a lawyer, then you don't have to read them their rights.

STUDENT: Is there anything on the books that says a person, while being tortured, can invoke the Fifth Amendment so he won't incriminate himself?

PROFESSOR: An intelligence officer will refuse to accept that because the United States Constitution doesn't apply to Iraqis or member of Al Queda.

STUDENT: So there is nothing in the Constitution about torture?

PROFESSOR: Not in so many words, but the founding fathers didn't reject using it against the British when we were fighting during the Revolutionary War.

STUDENT: What about the Geneva Convention?

PROFESSOR: Wash out your mouth with soap and water.

STUDENT: Where do the CIA, the Pentagon and the White House stand on torture?

PROFESSOR: They look to the Justice Department to tell them what they can do and can not do. In legal terms we say they are all protecting their derrieres.

STUDENT: Let's say a prisoner claims he has been arrested without reason.

PROFESSOR: The rule of thumb is a suspect is guilty until proven innocent.

STUDENT: Professor, after graduation I am going to sign up with a contractor who wants me to do intelligence work in Iraq. Will I be protected from congressional committees who want to know what I am doing there?

PROFESSOR: Yes. You don't have to answer any questions about torture because you are a civilian. That is why the Pentagon and CIA will pay you so well.

STUDENT: Several of the prison guards are awaiting court-martials for being bad apples in the military. How should we handle their trials?

PROFESSOR: The defense will maintain their clients were only following orders. As a friend of the court the Justice Department will say, "Okay, try them, and then let's sweep the rest of it under the rug."

STUDENT: Then it should not go up the chain of command?

PROFESSOR: No, because if it did it could land on the desk of the Secretary of Defense.

STUDENT: If we write a memorandum for the Justice Department stating torture may be justified for those who won't talk, do we have to disclose that we wrote it?

PROFESSOR: No way, because you have a lawyer-client relationship with the CIA and the Pentagon. In the case of Darkness vs. Misery, as a friend of the court, Ashcroft defended Darkness maintaining that the International Red Cross has nothing to say about torture if it is done in good faith. The thing you must remember is that we are at war and human rights are thrown out the window.

My time is up. There will be a test on Thursday. Your homework is to bring in any obscene pictures from the newspapers you can find.

The Rich are Different

IT IS ABOUT TIME somebody said something nice about the rich. The media, politicians and the middle and lower classes are constantly trashing them.

What are the rich really like? Rich people believe in God and country and tax cuts. They have homes in Manhattan, Palm Beach, Aspen, Malibu and Paris. They pay 15 million dollars for a house and 15 million more to fix it up so it will appear in *Architectural Digest*.

There are nouveau rich and there is old money. Donald Trump is a nouveau rich who puts his name on every building in the United States. He flies on jets and helicopters, and sails on yachts. He is a television star. On his television show he explains to fledgling executives how they can also get rich. Trump doesn't have to worry about joining a golf club. If he can't get in he'll build one.

Old money tries to stay out of the papers and magazines. The only time they get in is when a supermarket tabloid shows a picture of one of them topless at the beach in Capri.

What has happened recently is that the dress code has changed. The very rich people in Hollywood, New York and Silicon Valley show off their wealth by looking grungy. A torn tee-shirt and ripped Levis indicates how rich they really are. You can go to the finest restaurants if you are rich and they will let you in without a jacket or tie.

Rich women still dress up. They carry Prada handbags, wear Versace pantsuits in the daytime, and black Christian Dior dresses with pearls at night. They will pay $500 for Gucci sneakers.

Rich people order expensive wines even if they have no idea what they are drinking. They know the maitre d' by his first name and tip heavily so they won't get a bad table.

Rich people don't root for sports teams—they own them.

The one thing rich people have to suffer is crooked rich people who cheat, embezzle and steal from their own companies to get even richer than they already are. Although there are not many of these shady rich people (check the front pages every day), they give honest rich people a bad name.

The crooked rich, when caught, will defend themselves by saying, "Everybody does it." If they are worried about going to jail they will rat on their crooked rich friends in exchange for a plea bargain. Usually the government will allow them to keep their mansions and their wives can hold onto their diamond necklaces.

If there is any cloud in the happiness of rich people it is with their children. Some, not all, resent their parents being rich. They hate them because the parents buy them expensive cars and audio equipment and they finance spring break trips to Key West and Acapulco. Worst of all, much to the horror of their parents, some rich kids become Democrats and speak out against Bush's tax cuts.

Those who say rich people are just like you and me don't know what they are talking about. They have their lives and we have ours. The main difference is we have to take out our garbage, but the rich never see any.

In case you ever run into a rich person, don't be hostile. You can dream someday that you will be one of them and find the "Bluebird of Happiness."

Michael, Say It Isn't So

MICHAEL MOORE'S *Fahrenheit 9/11* opened last week at a glittery Hollywood preview in Washington. There was a red carpet, press, photographers and an elite audience of liberals, left-wingers, and as Michael said, "People who believe in freedom and are against those who are trying to take it away from them."

I was there, not as a liberal or an "anti-Busher," but as a fair and objective journalist, who will go to any movie if it is free and the popcorn is on the house.

As people walked down the carpet, the cameras whirled. Every network and cable station was there. My companion suggested we walk through with paper bags on our heads in case the FBI or the Republican Party were taking pictures.

Michael Moore arrived and a roar went up from the audience. He took the mike onstage and he said he knew he was talking to the choir of the converted, but since they were all asleep he wanted his film to wake them up. After a lengthy speech the house lights dimmed and the show was on.

Ever since then I have been asked what I thought of the film. I give it one-and-a-half thumbs and one pinky, and I'm not just saying this to get my loyal and revered conservative readers upset.

Did I think it was fair to the administration?

Of course not.

Did I think it gave a balanced picture of how we got bogged down in Iraq?

Of course not.

Was the relationship between the Bushes and the House of Saud any reason for Moore to make it a focal point of the story? Probably not, but it was only a film and should not be accepted as completely true any more than Mel Gibson's *The Passion of the Christ* should.

There were too many things in the movie that were overdone. Michael used every shot of the president playing golf that he could find. I think it slowed down the action and the only people who were interested were golfers.

In his film, Moore used a real commercial for Halliburton. I found it informative because a spokesman for Halliburton explained exactly what they do, which gives balance to the plot.

The funniest thing in the film was when Congressman Goss, Chairman of the House Committee on Intelligence, defended the Patriot Act and gave his telephone number out at a news conference to call if anyone thought his rights had been taken away. It turns out it was a phony number. As a practical joke Michael listed Goss's real telephone number in the film.

The Congressman didn't think it was as funny as Moore thought he would.

The film is rated R, which means children can't see it. But Harvey Weinstein, the executive producer, said the R stands for Republican.

You can either review *Fahrenheit 9/11* as a political tract or as entertainment, like *The Wizard of Oz*. Moore's backers say they intended the movie to be both. They hope the box office receipts will fly over the rainbow and also affect the election.

I'll be honest. I've never seen a picture like this and I am an addicted movie fan.

Should Michael Moore have made this film?

Yes, but only if he wanted to prove it is a free country.

To give you some idea where I stand, after the picture was over, I did not get up when Michael Moore got a standing ovation.

The Trial

"SADDAM HUSSEIN, please raise your left hand, the one we will chop off if we find you guilty of crimes too numerous to mention. Do you promise to tell the truth, the whole truth, and nothing but the truth so help you Allah?"

"I do."

"Mr. Hussein, you have committed many horrendous crimes, including murder, ethnic cleansing, gassing, and rape—and you have 2,300 unpaid traffic tickets in Baghdad. How do you plead?"

"Not guilty."

"How can you say that when the entire world has seen what you did?"

"My sons, Uday and Qusay, did all those things. You know how kids are."

"Didn't you know what they were doing?"

"I was suspicious that they were up to some mischief, but they were my sons, so I thought they would outgrow it."

"There is evidence that you killed a million Kurds. Why?"

"They pissed me off."

"Did you ever use poison gas to do it?"

"I didn't ask any questions. When it comes to genocide I always leave the decisions up to the generals in the field."

"I would like to ask you how you could build so many palaces on your salary as president."

"I was able to do it through the Food for Peace program. I provided the United Nations with oil in exchange for food. I took kickbacks on each barrel."

"Didn't you feel you were short-changing your people who were starving to death?"

"They never complained. If anyone did we would listen to his story and then shoot him."

Mr. Hussein, you are charged with rape. How many Iraqi women were your victims?"

"I don't remember."

"One hundred? Two hundred? Three hundred?"

"A lot more. But I was only following orders."

"Whose orders?"

"I forget the person's name, but I do know he was high up in the chain of command."

"Here is a picture of you firing a rifle on the presidential balcony. Weren't you violating your own anti-gun laws?"

"I had a permit."

"You couldn't have done all the things you are accused of alone. Please tell us the names of those who helped you."

"If I name names will it help me?"

"It might. We always show leniency towards those who will rat on their friends. Now I am going to show you a deck of cards with war criminals on them. Please pick a card. Who is that?"

"That's Chemical Ali. We called him that as a joke because he loved to gas Kurds. And that is Kamal Mustafa Abdallah al-Tikriti, my half brother. He tortured all my enemies regardless of race, color or profession."

"Take another card."

"That is Barzan Ibrahim al-Tikriti. He is another half brother and he played ball on the same little league soccer team as I did in Mosul. Would you like me to do card tricks? Take a card, any card, with a war criminal's face on it. Now put it back in the deck. The card you picked is Tariq Aziz, the deputy Prime Minister. Right?"

"May I continue the cross examination? Have you ever heard of the Abu Ghraib prison?"

"I've heard of it, but I have never been there."

"Why not?"

"It had a bad reputation, both before the invasion and then after. When I heard we tortured prisoners there I ordered an investigation, but before I could get a Red Cross report my statue was toppled."

"Mr. Hussein, do you feel that you did anything wrong?"

"If I did, I am saving it for my book."

"Oh Darn"

....

VICE PRESIDENT CHENEY said it and the whole world heard it. He told Senator Patrick Leahy to "F— yourself."

I hadn't heard this kind of talk since I watched *The Sopranos*.

Cheney said the words at a photo op, but the Senate wasn't in session, so he couldn't be penalized by the Democratic minority.

Let's discuss this like civilized people. The act is physically impossible. I assume Cheney knew this. If he told Leahy to "buzz off," or "go fly a kite," it would have been politically correct, even in an election year.

Since so many people heard it, it is possible that an intern might have slipped something in his herbal tea.

As a grandfather, I was upset that my four grandchildren heard about it. After it was reported in the papers, one of my grandsons told his brother what he could do to himself.

When I said, "Wash out your mouth with soap and water," he replied, "If Cheney can say it, so can I."

But fortunately, another grandson said, "I don't want to be president if you have to use foul language."

Since Cheney said it, the F-word has become part of our family's mantra.

One of the complaints about Vice President Cheney using obscenities is that he is just a heartbeat away from the presidency. He might just lose his cool when delivering a State of the Union speech.

Occasionally people do use the expression, but many say it under their breath when being chastised by their boss, or when arguing with someone who stole their parking space.

The Washington Post actually spelled out the word, something I have not seen before.

What effect will this have on foreign relations? Will the U.S. tell the French to do what Cheney told Leahy to do?

I heard that Colin Powell used the word in dealing with President Chirac. I called the State Department and the person who answered the phone laughed and said, "We've been telling the French to 'beep off' for years."

To our knowledge, President Bush has not publicly told anyone to F— himself, but a White House spokesperson said he tells friends to do it, like he used to at Yale.

Cheney says if the president uses such language then the vice president has to support him. We won't know how much Mr. Bush used the expression until we hear the tapes from the Oval Office.

Richard Nixon used the F-word the entire time he was in the White House.

Did George Washington use such cuss words? Historians say he didn't, but Andrew Jackson made it part of his vocabulary.

Lincoln didn't because he was too much of a gentleman.

But Teddy Roosevelt said it to prove how macho he was.

So what does this mean to the country?

It means what it says it means.

We have lost our moral compass. The Cheney people say to "bleep" is not bad if all the VP was really doing was wishing Senator Leahy a nice day.

It is a verb and you can conjugate it—I bleep, you bleep, we bleep.

I expect to hear quibbling about the word, but it is no big deal.

Telling another person to go "bleep" himself mainly because you don't like him is something we all do sooner or later. I have five people in mind right now, but I am not allowed to reveal their names.

How Many Wars?

THE BIG QUESTION that has come up is how many wars can we fight with our present military forces? The reason the issue has come to a boil is that the Pentagon is keeping the reserve troops in Iraq longer than they said they would have to be there.

The previous rule of thumb as to how many troops we need was how many wars we could fight at the same time.

Every president sees it differently. President Eisenhower believed nuclear weapons were enough of a deterrent to stop the soviets and any other enemy. His slogan was, "More bang for the buck."

John F. Kennedy was a two-and-a-half war president. He wanted us to be prepared to fight the Russians, the Chinese, and some third country, like Cuba.

When China and the Soviet Union stopped talking to each other, Kennedy scaled down our military strategy to one-and-a-half wars—assuming neither country would attack us at the same time.

At the beginning of his term, Lyndon Johnson was told by his secretary of defense, Robert McNamara, that we could get by fighting one-and-a-quarter wars—the quarter being Viet Nam. But before you could say "Ho Chi Minh," Viet Nam became a full-fledged war. So Johnson said he needed enough money to fight that war and also the one against the Soviet Union.

After Nixon made his trip to China, he thought he could get along with two wars, though there was some question about whether he could do it with a volunteer army.

President Carter came along and all his critics accused him of short-changing the country by giving the Pentagon funds for only one war. As a former captain of a nuclear submarine he said he knew more about war than most people.

President Reagan, who was known as a peacemaker, said we must prepare for a nuclear war, a conventional war, and a "protracted" war—and still have enough armed forces to invade Grenada.

The "Great Communicator" also asked for money to build a "Star Wars" defense, and was so convincing Congress gave it to him. Reagan claimed that even if his Strategic Defense Initiative didn't work, the Soviets would think it did and go bankrupt trying to duplicate it.

He was right, because the Kremlin threw out communism with the bath water, and Reagan is still getting full credit for it.

George Bush the First decided to stop Iraq from overtaking Kuwait. That was known as the Gulf War—except the U.S. never laid a glove on Saddam Hussein.

Bill Clinton was not sure how many wars he wanted to get into. He was criticized for this, but he had other things on his mind.

Now we come to the present George Bush. He told his Secretary of Defense that he wanted the world to know the United States was not to be trifled with.

Rumsfeld said he would produce a mean and lean military that could fight anywhere and any time, and still give everyone a tax cut.

The president accepted the word of the Pentagon and based his foreign policy on war. Bush differs from other presidents in that he felt it was legal to attack the enemy before the enemy attacked us—particularly after the CIA told Bush that Iraq had weapons of mass destruction.

Bush told the country, "War, in the cause of peace, is no disgrace."

His plans went awry when people like Ahmed Chalabi assured everyone that invading Iraq was a piece of cake.

Based on this and other misinformation, the Pentagon alerted all its troops and mobilized the National Guard. The invasion was obviously not a piece of cake and to this day nobody can tell us how long our troops will remain there.

How many wars can America have at one time? Knows only God.

Commissions for Boo-Boos

WHENEVER SOMEONE in the administration makes a boo-boo and the public finds out about it, an announcement is made that two commissions are being set up. One commission is formed to find out what went wrong and another to find out who leaked the boo-boo to the press.

There are now more commissions and investigating committees in Washington than there is office space to accommodate them.

The reason for all these commissions is that after the administration commits a blooper it is buying time—first by forming the committee, and second by waiting for it to make a report. When that finally happens, they hope the reason for appointing the commission will have been forgotten. (See any environmental commission.)

Even when appointing a commission, the White House can blow it. Pressure was on President Bush to find out why 9/11 was allowed to happen. At first he refused, but then finally agreed to create a commission. To make sure it would be a friendly one, he announced Henry Kissinger would be the chair, but Kissinger said he would only take the job if he didn't have to reveal the names of his multi-billionaire clients.

The Democrats and the press didn't think it was such a good idea because hearings conducted by Kissinger would not embarrass the government.

It wasn't a big loss for Henry. Thanks to all the publicity, he signed up more new clients after he withdrew his name.

This points out how difficult it is to find a few good men who are politically acceptable to serve and who won't overturn the apple cart by calling President Bush, Vice President Cheney,

Donald Rumsfeld, Colin Powell, and Condoleezza Rice to testify. (See any commission hearings.)

Sometimes the commission will ask to see the documents pertaining to the hearings. The White House will agree, if they can find them, or refuse by pleading executive privilege. (See Vice President Cheney's energy task force meeting notes.)

The administration takes far more seriously uncovering who has leaked the blooper to the press. Teams of FBI agents are put on the case and not only the leaker, but also all the reporters involved are questioned. The Bush people are still trying to find out who leaked the name of a top secret CIA agent to Robert Novak. There are some people who say the leaker has an office in the White House and did it to embarrass the person who was embarrassing the president. (See Richard Clarke.)

Leaking is a dirty business, but someone has to do it.

There are now so many FBI agents looking for so many leakers that they can't do their other jobs—like investigate people who are illegally recording movies and music. (See Jack Valenti.)

Members of the Senate and House also set up committees to find out what went wrong, particularly if they can get on television. Republicans and Democrats differ on what questions to ask the witnesses. (See Abu Ghraib prison photo hearings).

So, as each committee and commission is formed, the unemployment rate for people in Washington goes down. Nobody knows how many people will be needed to sit on future panels, but it will probably double because it is an election year.

The big question you are asking is what happens to all the presidential commission reports after they are handed in? (See *The 9/11 Commission Report*.)

Most of them will be marked "Top Secret" and shredded—or placed in an unmarked grave at Camp David.

Image Control

IT WAS A FUNNY HEADLINE: "Drug Companies Seek to Mend Their Image." The question was, what image?

Apparently the pharmaceutical companies decided that the customer was beginning to think they were only interested in raising prices, making barrels of money, and producing very expensive TV commercials.

The top manufacturers met to figure out a way to bring back the good will they used to have in days of yore.

Malaprop, President of Outrageous Profit Pharmaceuticals, said, "The people are starting to believe we are too greedy and are only interested in the bottom line."

"Well put," said Dormer, of Drugs-R-Us. "We have to change our image. Our polls show people think we are responsible for many people dying because they can't afford our drugs."

Shortstop, the lobbyist for Hysdranstan Drugs, said, "If we don't change our image, Congress will listen to the people who elected them instead of to us."

"Even if we give them more money for their political campaigns?"

"Yes," said Shortstop. "The people who are causing us the most trouble are members of the media. Yet without our full-page ads and TV commercials they are out of business."

Gladstern, marketing head for Rough Pharmaceuticals, said, "We have our people visiting doctor's offices with samples of our products and offering them cruises to Bermuda and family weekends at Disney World if they prescribe our drugs. Why can't we send our representatives into newspaper offices and TV stations to offer free samples of our erectile dysfunction pills?"

Shortstop said, "It would be worth a try. A lot of newspaper men are suffering from it."

"We should tell the public that our stockholders are widows and orphans."

"And they are people who depend on our company dividends for their pensions."

Dormer said, "The reason we have such a bad image is that people know it is much cheaper to buy our drugs in Canada."

Shortstop said, "Our lobbyists are working on that right now. There is a bill pending in congress that has the president's support which forbids imports of pharmaceuticals from other countries and generic drugs. We think it is a slam dunk."

Malaprop said, "The ones who always complain about prices are senior citizens."

Gladstern agreed. "They complain about everything. Even my mother called me a serial pill gouger the other day."

"Don't senior citizens understand how capitalism works?" Shortstop asked.

"We have to make it much clearer. I suggest a commercial showing white rats playing in their cages. A man in a white jacket says, 'Each rat costs us two dollars, but we don't mind spending the money if it will help our research find a new pill to cure athlete's foot.'"

"It should fly," said Dormer. "We could also do another TV ad. It would show an elderly couple with white hair surfing in Hawaii. As they come out of the water holding a surfboard the husband says, 'Thanks to Whizbottom I feel like a new man.' His wife winks and says, 'He is a new man. Jerry has found the perfect pill for the perfect wave.' Then a voiceover will say, 'Warning, Whizbottom may cause nausea, high blood pressure, tingling in your feet, shortness of breath, dizziness, and should not be taken when driving a bulldozer.' Then the couple dives back into the ocean."

Malaprop said, "If we are really sincere we can win back the hearts and minds of our customers. But we have to double our public relations budget."

Shortstop asked, "Can we afford it?"

"Malaprop replied, "We can if we double the price of our drugs."

Couch Potatoes

....

NOVEMBER'S ELECTION will not be decided by the people who attended the conventions. It will be decided by the couch potatoes who stayed at home.

I have to admit that I am a couch potato. I watched the Democratic Convention last week with six friends at the Lucas house. Nadia Lucas had laid out guacamole, cheese dip, tacos, and popcorn, which all couch potatoes consider comfort food.

"Quiet everyone. Did you hear what I heard?"

"What?"

"Theresa Kerry told a newspaper writer to 'Shove it.'"

"She is going to get my vote."

"You didn't say anything when Dick Cheney said to Senator Leahy, 'Go f— yourself.'"

"He is a man and he is entitled to say anything he wants. A woman must be more ladylike if she hopes to be the First Lady."

"I still say she has won the 'Shove it' vote, particularly amongst women who believe they are not getting a fair break."

People started digging into the guacamole.

"Boy, all the speeches are downbeat about what is going on in this country. They keep saying the rich get all the cake and the poor just get the crumbs."

"The speakers have to say something to get a standing ovation. They want the delegates to wave their signs and clap their hands and shout 'Kerry!'"

The Republicans will do the same thing. You can't have a convention without standing ovations."

"I wish everybody wouldn't say that we are worse off today than we were four years ago. I sell handbags and the speakers are not helping my business."

"Every speaker brings up Kerry's war record."

"Why not? Bush has none."

"That's dirty pool. The president didn't fly in the war but he landed on a carrier after we won in Iraq."

"I don't think the Democrats should keep pointing to the fact that there were no weapons of mass destruction in Iraq. We went there to wipe out Saddam Hussein and we did a good job."

"It seems to me that they are hitting the 'job' problem too hard. Every time a speaker says the unemployment rate is at its highest, the applause is thunderous."

"They are not cheering the unemployment rate—they are cheering the people who are responsible for it."

The cheese dish was getting low.

"The Kerry girls are very pretty."

"You don't vote for a president because he has pretty daughters. Bush's daughters are beautiful, too."

"Anyone seen a poll on whose daughters are more beautiful?"

"Clinton is a rock star."

"So is Bono."

"Michael Moore and Bill O'Reilly went mano a mano the other night on Fox. It was the best show of the night because they weren't kidding. I would give it to Moore on points."

And so it went. The couch potatoes for the most part are still in the "don't know" column. They say they're waiting to see if Laura Bush will tell someone at her convention to "Shove it."

Meat Loaf

EVERY SUMMER there is a story that blows my mind. This summer the big news is that my friend Mike Wallace was arrested in New York and was handcuffed and taken to the slammer.

Let's get the facts straight. Mike drove to a take-out restaurant on Third Avenue for meat loaf. The traffic police said his driver was double-parked. (Mike does not drive in New York because he can never find a place to park without paying $20 an hour.)

Mike, who was hungry, went into the take-out. When he came out he saw that the traffic police were saying unkind things to his driver. Mike intervened and was told to get back in his limo. When he refused, Mike exchanged unkind words with the police. They say he lunged at them. Mike says he has never lunged at anyone in his life, including Barbra Streisand.

The next thing you know he was handcuffed and taken to the station house. The press went crazy, and as far as I can tell, they are still in a shark frenzy.

Mike has given his side of the story to every newscaster on the air. Now those are the facts.

I have known Mike Wallace for years, and although he cheats at tennis, I have never known him to double-park in New York. The only time he committed "disorderly conduct" was when he tried a junk shot on the court.

Why the public's interest? Mike is an American icon. He has interviewed China's leaders, Saudi Arabian sheiks and exposed healthcare scams in Florida. Every Sunday millions of people sit in their living rooms waiting for their *60 Minutes* fix.

Mike speaks for the little people. If someone is in jail, Mike tries to get him out, and if a crook is not in jail, he tries to send him there.

So the reason there was such a stir when Mike got arrested was because he was handcuffed. People who have double-parked were on his side. Those who admire him for his looks considered him a role model. Those who love take-out food said they would do the same thing.

I know Mike Wallace from Martha's Vineyard. I have been in his home, played gin rummy with him, and eaten lobster with him.

But he did break the law.

The question everyone must answer is one of loyalty. Do you stand with the person who double-parked and says he will never do it again—or do you let the wheels of justice turn?

I have chosen to stand by Mike. If he needs it I will even start a "Free Mike Wallace" fund. I am planning a parade down Third Avenue if I can get a permit and a parking place.

Mike is now back on the Vineyard, awaiting his trial in October. They didn't make him put up any bail or give up his passport. (Brazil is the only country that does not consider double-parking an extraditable offense.) CBS guaranteed he would not skip the country.

Now you know the whole story. Some good things came out of it. Mayor Bloomberg declared meat loaf the official New York comfort food. Mike now wears a sweatshirt that says, "Doubleparkers Need Love Too," and he has been nominated for the "Parking Hall of Fame."

Husseinku

HERE'S THE LATEST NEWS about Saddam. He's in jail being given three healthy meals a day, is allowed to garden, read books, and write poetry.

This is the verse I think he would write. It is called Husseinku.

Allah is good,
Allah is merciful,
Allah kills worms in my garden.

My two sons are gone,
Gone to heaven,
Does that mean we can't win the Olympics?

If I killed any Kurds
It was for their own good.
Poison gas is cheap.

People say I am evil,
People say I am bad,
But why do people hate me?

It will take two years to try me.
Not to worry,

I will plead insanity.

If I don't have a hung jury
I will get my people
To hang the jury.

The Red Cross brings me shaving cream,
The Red Cross brings me Marlboros,
Yet they know I smoke Camels.

I am happy because
Although I am here,
My money is in Switzerland.

Osama is still free.
If he turned himself in
He would get three hot meals a day.

My prison guards are soldiers
Who keep looking at me
To make sure I am me.

My wives don't come to visit me.
If they get married again,
I won't give them child support.

I don't believe in women's rights.
I don't believe in same-sex marriage.
Call me a conservative.

I miss my shotgun,

I miss my pheasants,
I miss my bodyguards who miss me.

They won't let me be on TV.
Who can it hurt,
But Larry King?

When I die seventy-two virgins wait for me.
It will be hard to remember
All their names.

I am willing to do community service
As long as it doesn't
Hurt my back.

They tore my statue down.
It wasn't me.
It was one of my doubles.

I am a prisoner of war,
They can't yell at me,
Or make me take off all my clothes.

I can't spit on Iran,
I can't spit on the U.S.,
I am in a "No spitting" zone.

Give my regards to Kuwait,
Say hello to Mosul Square,
Tell the boys I will soon be there.

After killing a spider
I feel better because
I have killed before.

The sand blows in my face,
Bush can't find my weapons,
So he just sucks on hard candies.

In addition to his poetry, Saddam also writes books. He lives a good life—and that is why we invaded Iraq.

Compassionate Conservatism

AT THEIR CONVENTION, the Republicans' main theme was "Compassionate Conservatism." The party wanted the world to know they care for the poor, children, the environment, and the war in Iraq.

How did they achieve their goal?

I talked to doctor Heinrich Applebaum, the party's medical advisor. I said, "We all know the Republican platform was much farther to the right than the speakers. What was their secret?"

"I gave them Compassionate Conservative pills," he said. "Just before they went up on the stage they took two pills with a glass of water. If they felt the effects were wearing off, they took two more while they were speaking."

"After taking the pills could they drive or use heavy equipment?"

"I warned them it was not such a good idea."

"The people at the convention didn't mind the compassion?"

"No. Even the right wing cheered the early speakers because they knew the last two nights they would get red meat," he said.

"By the way, what is a Compassionate Conservative?"

"It is someone who believes he wants to help the working poor, the uneducated, and the unemployed—not with money, but with prayers and tax cuts."

"Amen," I said.

"This is the opposite of the liberal who is the enemy of the state and wants the government to bail out the country. The liberal is against drilling for oil in Alaska, cutting down trees in Oregon and limiting the number of snowmobiles in Yellowstone National Park."

"What about Dick Cheney?"

"He refused to take any. He said the pills made him nauseous. He told us beforehand he was not going to play the role of the good guy. The vice president doesn't have to be a Compassionate Conservative. He has to say things with no compassion at all."

"He made his point in his speech to the choir," I agreed. "I noticed he didn't defend his role in Halliburton."

"He felt the convention wasn't the right place to do it and the press would have another excuse to make a big deal over it."

What about Senator Zell Miller, the Democrat from Georgia who gave the Republican keynote speech?"

"Because it was such an extreme switch, the pills didn't work. We had a cardiologist give him a heart transplant. Since he gave the keynote speech for Clinton in 1992, he needed a new heart."

"You did a marvelous job," I told him. "He sounded more like a Republican than Dick Cheney. He said he didn't leave the Democratic Party—it left him. Did you give Arnold Schwarzenegger a heart transplant?"

"Yes. His was one of the most successful Compassionate Conservative heart operations we have had."

"Whose heart did you give him?"

Applebaum replied, "If you promise not to tell anyone, we gave him Teddy Kennedy's."

"I don't believe it."

"Figure it out. Arnold is married to Maria Shriver, a member of the Kennedy family."

"But Teddy is a liberal. What is his heart doing in a Republican's body?"

"Arnold does not agree with everything in the Republican Party, but his heart still belongs to Bush."

"But when he spoke he sounded like a liberal. How could he agree to the transplant?"

"Maria told him, 'You owe it to our family.'"

Left Behind

I KNOW YOU WON'T BELIEVE THIS, but in spite of what Bush said, I met a child who was left behind. He was sitting on the curb, crying.

"What are you crying about?"

"I was left behind."

"Where are your parents?"

"My mother is in a rehab home and I don't know who my father is. I can't read or write and everyone makes fun of me."

"That shouldn't be. The president said he didn't want to leave one child behind."

"What is a president?"

"He is not God, but he thinks he is. He claims to produce miracles and he loves all his children."

"I never saw him."

"He is there. You are very important to his educational program, and if anyone finds that you are left behind it could hurt him in the November election. Why do you think you were left behind?"

"The teacher didn't like me."

"I am sure you made that up."

"I didn't have nice clothes and everyone else said I was a troublemaker. The teacher said if I didn't keep quiet she would leave me behind."

"That must have frightened you."

"Not really. She has left behind hundreds, maybe thousands."

"Well, you are the only one I know sitting on the curb crying."

"The others are hanging out at the street corner or stealing hub caps and anything else they can get their hands on."

"Wait until the president finds out. He will turn Homeland Security on them. Has anyone told you that you were left behind?"

"No one talks to me so how would I know?"

"Well, you must have felt it or you wouldn't be crying."

"What does it all mean?"

"It all started when the Children's Defense Fund used 'Leave No Child Behind' as its slogan. Then President Bush stole the idea and used 'No Child Left Behind' as his slogan. Now he says he will see that no one is left behind, even though he knows it is not the truth."

The child looked at me blankly.

I continued, "It is all political. The president wants everyone to think he cares about them. Then they will vote for him."

"If he really cared about me he would buy me basketball sneakers."

"He can't afford that. He has a war to fight."

The boy started crying again.

I said, "If I bought you sneakers would you stop crying and go back to school?"

"Uh-huh—the ones like Michael Jordan wears."

"Maybe, but you have to promise to go back to school and study."

"How can I study if I can't read or write?"

"You are going to have to learn. Otherwise you will be left behind again and you will eventually wind up snatching purses from ladies as they are walking down the street."

"They will never catch me if I have Michael Jordan's sneakers."

"No sneakers no school."

"Why are you talking to me?"

"You are the only child I have met who has been left behind. You are a good human interest story."

He thought about this. "Will you buy me a Big Mac?"

"For a kid you drive a hard bargain. I will, but I'm not doing it for you—I'm doing it for President Bush."

Trial Lawyers—Who Needs Them?

ONE OF THE BIGGEST standing ovations at the recent Republican convention occurred when the speaker attacked trial lawyers because they are driving up the cost of healthcare with their malpractice lawsuits.

It was a dangerous move because there is now a lawyer in every household and I have one in my family. She was watching the convention with me on television in the living room.

She said, "What do they know about malpractice? They are not telling the truth, the whole truth, and nothing but the truth, so help them God."

"But it is good politics," I said.

"I had a case where a surgeon removed the wrong breast from a patient. Another doctor had to remove the correct breast. If anyone ever needed a trial lawyer she did."

I was appalled.

She said, "It wasn't just a question of money. My client wanted to put the doctor out of business so he would never operate again."

She continued, "Now here is the rotten part of it. The insurance company representing the doctor also had a trial lawyer. He tried to blacken her name to the jury and prove my client was responsible for what happened.

"So trial lawyers are not only hired to bring malpractice suits, they are also signed up as defense lawyers by doctors and drug companies. The lobbyists in Washington want Congress to put a cap on the amount of money awarded in suits that would punish doctors and drug companies."

"I have never met a lobbyist who didn't get what he wanted," I said.

She continued, "Trial lawyers don't just do malpractice cases. They also defend people accused of white-collar crimes. I bet there are a lot of them in the hall right now."

"How do you know?"

"They are the ones sitting on their hands when everyone else is on their feet cheering the attacks on lawyers."

"I can see why they could be upset."

"The law is the trial lawyers' bread and butter. They will not only defend Republicans, but Democrats as well if the fee is right," she said. "And in class action suits they will charge whatever the traffic will bear."

"Is the reason the Republicans don't like John Edwards because he made so much money as a trial lawyer?"

"They say that, but the truth is, when anyone gets in trouble the first person they call is a lawyer. I only wish I had the legal fees of Martha Stewart, Ken Lay, Kobe Bryant and any bank accused of getting in trouble with the government."

"Are government lawyers also members of the trial lawyer profession?"

"Yes, if they are any good. And when they leave the government they represent the side they prosecuted."

She asked, "Did you know that if trial lawyers were forbidden to practice there would be no courtroom television shows?"

"Do people who are booing trial lawyers also hate people who serve on juries?"

"They do if the jurors award the plaintiffs more than $500,000, or whatever the cap would be. The country needs doctors, preferably those who don't make mistakes. But it also needs lawyers in case they do."

"Then this demonstration does not bother you?"

"Not as long as Congress is made up of lawyers."

Do It Our Way

....

WE HAVE BEEN INFORMED that, come January, the democratic people of Iraq are going to have elections. This is the first election in their history and they don't know how to hold one.

A representative from "Shrek," one of the Iraqi political parties, came to Washington to learn some pointers from the American elections.

He met with an American election expert in Washington who told him, "The first thing your candidate has to do is learn to lie."

"Iraqis never lie,"

"You are going to have to learn. We would never hold an election if American candidates didn't lie. Now the wonderful thing about American politics is if you keep repeating the lie often enough you will start believing it yourself. And if the voters feel that you believe it they will believe it."

"I am taking notes."

"You have to hit below the belt."

"Moslems don't have belts."

"Never mind. Say that if the people don't vote for your candidate the other side will bring Saddam back to power and the terrorists will take over the country."

"Does my candidate have to apologize after he says it?"

"Of course not. The object of winning an election is to scare the hell out of the electorate."

"What about gun control? Should our candidate be for it or against it?"

"He must declare that under the Iraqi Constitution everyone has a right to a gun."

"But we have no constitution."

"When you get one you will have the right to bear arms. In the meantime, your boy will say every citizen has a duty to keep one under his pillow."

"That won't be an issue in Iraq."

"Where was your man during the first Gulf War?"

"He was in the Iraqi National Guard in Morocco."

"Your opposition is going to try to make that an issue."

"What should my man say?"

"He must say he served honorably and he has his dental records to prove it."

"What about television ads?"

"That is where you want to spend your money. Tell the people that your opposition threw his medals into the Tigris."

"We don't have any money for TV."

"The CIA will give you all you want. After all, it is to the United States' advantage that you hold free elections."

"What are the big issues we should concentrate on?"

"Security is number one."

"But they are still fighting in Fallujah, Tikrit and Baghdad."

"Deny it. Always deny. After security, your people will be interested in jobs. Fifty percent of all Iraqis are out of work. Promise them that you will create three thousand new jobs to rebuild the cities. Once again, the United States will supply the dollars and the jobs through Halliburton."

"Will you also pay for election bumper stickers?"

"Not only will we pay for them, but we will put them on our own tanks."

"What about the media?"

"The United States will provide you with enough spin to win the election."

"You have been very helpful, sir. May Allah bless you."

The Dan Rather Factor

LIKE IT OR NOT, I have to deal with the "Dan Rather Factor." It is important because Dan presented memos on *60 Minutes II* written by a colonel concerning his opinion as to how George W. Bush behaved in the Air National Guard. The memos have been questioned and might be forgeries.

This is what we know so far. Bush served honorably, but out of harm's way, in Alabama. Dan did not serve in the National Guard, but was in harm's way all that time.

We don't know where George was for six months of his service—and the White House won't tell us.

According to the colonel's memorandums, which could be forgeries, Bush refused to obey orders and had a "bad attitude." Colonel Killian, who has gone to that big Air National Guard in the sky, said the future president could not qualify to fly jet planes because he did not show up for his physical. Killian's secretary, who did all the colonel's typing, said she didn't type the memos, though she told Dan they were the colonel's thoughts.

Handwriting experts hired by CBS said they warned Rather that the documents might not be kosher. The question raised was whether the notes were made on an IBM Selectric or with word processing software at a Kinko's in Abilene, Texas. What makes the story more interesting is it turns out that nobody from the *60 Minutes II* staff has ever been in Abilene. Dan said, after questions hit the fan, that he intended to get to the bottom of his broadcast. Apparently he did and the bottom was that the documents were forged.

The questions they had to answer were:

What kind of officer was George Bush in the Air National Guard?

Did he really lean on his father's contacts to stay out of Vietnam?

Did John Kerry ever forge any papers to get his medals?

As commander-in-chief can Bush order Dan Rather to go to Iraq?

How will this affect CBS's *Survivor* ratings?

What if Kitty Kelley was wrong about George Bush snorting cocaine at Camp David?

What is the connection between Dan Rather, Kitty Kelley, and Martha Stewart?

As you can see, *60 Minutes II* opened up a whole can of beans, or as we say in Texas, the whole enchilada. At the beginning, I was on Dan's side—then I switched to Kinko's.

Every time there is a new charge concerning George's service in the Guard, the Pentagon "finds" a new piece of paper in its files showing Bush was one heckuva flyer. The last was a letter from George the First to Dubya's commanding officer thanking him for writing to tell him what an outstanding pilot his son was.

How will all this affect the elections? Nobody knows. I am not going to vote based on whether Dan Rather got suckered by someone who didn't like George Bush. I know it will not be an issue because nobody cares where the next president of the United States served.

But if he wins, don't expect George Bush to invite Dan Rather for dinner.

Our Long Nightmare Is Over Once Again

THE FCC HAS FINALLY put a price on a woman's breast. It is $550,000.

What happened, as EVERYBODY knows, was that Janet Jackson showed one of her breasts at half time during the Super Bowl. Eight hundred million people (including China) were horrified. No one had ever seen a woman's breast before, except in *National Geographic* magazine.

The reaction was tremendous. Mothers blindfolded their children; husbands turned off their TV sets and never saw the second half of the game.

How could a major network allow the full display of a body part, including a nipple, for all the public to see? More indignant calls came into the network than when Bush decided to invade Iraq. The FCC had no choice but to deal with it.

The problem was, no one at the agency had ever seen a bare breast before. This was cold flesh.

The meeting to fine CBS was held in FCC headquarters. There was a large screen TV at one end of the room. The commissioners were nervous.

"Do we have to see it?" one of them asked.

"Yes," the chairman replied. "It is our duty to protect every man, woman, and child in America."

"We didn't get any calls from men," a commissioner pointed out.

"It doesn't matter. A breast is still a breast. Roll 'em."

Janet Jackson came on the screen during halftime festivities, and suddenly, while she sang with Justin Timberlake, her shoulder strap snapped. It was only a few seconds, but it seemed like a lifetime.

"Play it again," a commissioner said. "This time close in on her."

It was obvious to everyone in the room that there was something wrong with the dress.

"We should fine the costume designer," someone said.

They played the smoking gun ten more times.

Then a commissioner said, "I am not saying it is so, but suppose it was no accident?"

The room was silent. "Why would any pop singer show her breast in public?"

"To sell her records and be talked about on every radio show in America."

"If this is true then CBS allowed it to happen."

"And should be fined so they never do it again."

A commissioner said, "It will prove to the world we are a moral nation."

"What we are saying if you allow one of your stars to rip her dress off is that you are going to have to pay the piper."

"But how much should we fine the network?"

"Five hundred and fifty thousand dollars."

"That is very harsh."

"It sends a message to any entertainer that the people who watch the *Super Bowl* are very fragile, and we, the FCC, took an oath to protect them."

"Play it again to make sure we are not making a mistake."

The meeting was adjourned. Where are Janet and CBS now? Janet Jackson is more in demand than ever before, and gives concerts when she isn't attending her brother Michael's trial.

CBS is now dealing with the Dan Rather brouhaha, and has proven Janet's breasts are her own and not forgeries.

Congressional No Flu Zone

THIS IS A HYPOTHETICAL QUESTION. There is a shortage of flu vaccine and you only have enough for one person. You have to decide between a congressman and your mother. Who gets the shot?

The answer, of course, is your congressman. The reason is, you can't do without your legislator, but you always can get another mother.

I know it is only a hypothetical question and it would never happen in America. On the other hand, the Capitol's attending physician recommended all 535 lawmakers and members of their staffs get a shot.

While as a senior citizen you might have to stand in line for hours at a Wal-Mart, all you have to do on the Hill is show your ID card—and "zap" or "prick."

When questions arose, it was explained that politicians have to shake more hands than any other group of people, and are more likely to catch the bug than forest rangers or fly fishermen. Thus, they would get sick and not pass the laws the country so desperately needs.

There are guidelines put out by the CDC which specifically say that the vaccine should go to babies under two years and people over sixty-five, as well as those in high risk groups.

Now the "high risk" category is the one that congress is banking on to defend why they should get the shots. Many people consider their lawmakers at high risk, particularly when it comes to adding so much pork to their bills.

Don't believe that your government is not facing up to the problem. They are suggesting you wash your hands as often as you can—and shake as few hands as possible. We keep seeing the candidates out there shaking hands with the masses, but we don't see their handlers off-camera with a bucket of soap and water so they can wash hands after each stop.

It is no secret that some people are steamed up about Congress jumping the line—or having no line at all.

One congressman said, "To refuse a flu shot when offered to you is the same thing as not taking a tax cut that your government wants to give you. Don't think it was easy for me to decide to get a shot. But then I had to think of my constituents. If I didn't get the vaccine and got sick, I couldn't look after their interests."

What makes the playing field uneven is that only incumbents can get a flu shot. This puts their opponents at a disadvantage.

It has become a major political issue. The incumbent is asking, "Do you want someone to represent you who is safe from disease, or someone who could wind up in the hospital at any time?"

The vaccine shortage did not hit people hard until they read about Congress being given all it wanted. Senate Majority Leader, Bill Frist, a doctor himself, told everyone on the Hill he thought it was a good idea to be vaccinated.

President Bush did not take his shot, but he was "working hard, very hard" on the problem. Finding flu vaccine when there is a shortage is "hard."

But Bush has a plan. He says we should stay the course and buy as much vaccine as we can from Canada.

What advice do I have for you, dear reader? Wash your hands.

Slam Dunk

....

BASKETBALL HAS ALWAYS BEEN a contact sport, with two teams in the heat of battle going against each other. Recently, as you have probably seen on television, the players went into the stand and started slugging the fans.

The Indiana Pacers won a close one, knocking down three Detroit Piston fans in the second row.

Fighting is part of the sport and the owners of basketball teams are constantly looking for players who are good with their hands—not necessarily with a ball.

Harvey Charger, one of the best sports agents in the business, called the owner of the Rustics and said, "Matty, I think I have a center for you. He is the best player in the league and he has just become a free agent."

Matty says, "I can use a good center. When can he start playing?"

"Next year."

"Next year?"

"He has been suspended this season for hitting a fan with a chair."

"If I sign him up how much do you want for him?"

"One million dollars, plus a $500,000 bonus."

"What is the bonus for?"

"Lawyers fees in case he is indicted for aggravated assault."

"How can I be sure he won't go into the stands again?"

"I give you my word. He will only hit a fan if he is provoked."

"Okay, I am willing to take a chance."

Harvey next called the owner of a National Football League team.

"Mike," he said, "the draft is coming up and I have an outstanding college football player for you."

"Who is he?"

"He is the Clemson guy in the middle of the pack who was swinging at a lineman from the University of South Carolina and hit a referee by mistake. It was on all the news shows. He will be the first draft choice, but if you are willing to deal I'll get him for you in exchange for the three linemen on your team who got thrown out of the Dallas game last week."

"Let me look at the films of the Clemson game again."

"Don't take too long. Everyone in the league wants him."

Mike said, "Okay, I could use a player that hits another player when the officials aren't looking."

Harvey hung up and yelled to his secretary, "Did you get me the manager of the Washington Nationals?"

"He's on line one."

Harvey picked up the phone and said, "Mr. Rebock, congratulations on coming to Washington. I know you are putting together your team and are looking for outstanding players. I have a shortstop who can hit right and left handed."

"I already have a shortstop."

"Not one who will attack the pitcher if he almost throws a ball at his head. The beauty of Morales is he doesn't speak any English so he doesn't know that in baseball you are not supposed to hit another player."

"Why don't you sell him to George Steinbrenner?"

"He is too cheap when it comes to salaries."

"I want to make sure the rest of my players come off the bench to join him if he gets into a fight."

Harvey said, "Gotcha."

He hangs up and talks to his partner.

"Do golfers fight much?"

"They would if there was enough money in it."

Crate and Baghdad

OF ALL THE WORDS that Colin Powell will be remembered for during his tenure as Secretary of State, the most memorable were the ones he said when President Bush told him he was going to invade Iraq. Powell said, "You break it, you own it."

The other day I went to the Crate and Baghdad store in Pentagon City. There was broken china and glass everywhere. The manager was sweeping it up.

"What happened?"

"A shopper came into the store, dropped one vase, then another, and kept on breaking everything in the shop."

"How much damage did he do?" I asked.

"One hundred and fifty billions dollars' worth, but the customer said he was going to come back for more."

"It looks like he did a lot of damage."

"The funny part is when he first came he said he wasn't going to break anything. He seemed like a good customer, so we showed him everything we had on display. But as soon as he bought something he dropped it. I told him it is our policy that if you break it you have to pay for it."

"Why do you think he keeps dropping things?"

"He can't hold anything in his hands. Instead of walking out of the store with a lot of expensive things, he leaves them in pieces on the floor."

"Does he come in alone?"

"No, he comes in with an entourage, and what he doesn't break, they do."

"You must be nervous when they come into the store."

"Not really, as long as they pay for everything."

"Then you don't care what they do?"

"It is good for business. We are having a sale right now—if you break one, you can break another one for free."

"That's a good pitch. When will the sale be over?"

"God only knows."

"Can you order on the Internet?"

"No," he said.

"Why not?" I asked.

"You can't break things from a computer."

The manager kept sweeping up the floor. He said, "Crate and Baghdad is the closest store to the Pentagon, and we stay open twenty-four hours a day. We have valet parking for generals, and a reserved spot for the secretary of defense, who is our best customer."

"Tell me about some of the things they have broken."

"China, glass chandeliers, mirrors, antiques, and they even have cut up Persian rugs."

"What do you keep on the back lot?"

"Hummers, tanks, armored trucks and Boeing airplanes."

"They can't be broken."

"Yes. When someone comes into our shop we take them to the back lot. Once we get them in the shop we can sell them anything their hearts desire."

"Are you thinking of expanding?"

"We have to. The more they buy the more they break."

"Do they pay cash?"

"No, they buy everything on credit."

"Who eventually pays for all the broken stuff?"

He smiled, "You do."

In God We Trust

....

LIKE ALL AMERICANS, I worship the U.S. dollar. I always believed it was the single thing that separated us from the rest of the world.

With the dollar you could travel anywhere and merchants would be happy to relieve you of it. Currencies in the rest of the world would fluctuate, but the mighty dollar stood firm.

Ugly American tourists in Europe would make snide remarks about the French franc and compare the Italian lire to Kleenex.

Everywhere they went there were signs in the store windows, "English Spoken—Dollars Welcome. Owner Willing to Take the Abuse."

American tourists pretended they were superior to the culture of "Old Europe." We were the new Empire and we made sure everyone knew it. I remember buying an English-French dictionary in Paris. The first thing you were supposed to say to a French merchant was, "How much is that in dollars?" The second thing you said was, "You are a crook."

It wasn't until 1957 that we printed "In God We Trust" on our greenbacks. We always knew God was behind the dollar, but we wanted to make sure the Communists knew it.

There were a few Americans who claimed that by putting God on our currency we were mixing church and state. But they lost the battle. From then on the whole world knew that God supported our currency. In order to attract people, the credit card companies put out the word that God also supported plastic, which was the same thing as dollars.

Obviously, the more dollars you had, the happier you were. Also, for some reason, the more you had, the less you had to pay. The American Dream was up there with God and Country.

Why am I prattling like this?

Out of the blue, the dollar is now dropping and the euro is going up.

The U.S. laughed when the euro first came out, but it isn't laughing anymore. To fight back we printed more money, but the more we printed, the more the dollar went down hill.

European merchants took down their "English Spoken Here" signs. A cup of coffee now costs five American dollars. Postcards are $30, and a gondola in Venice goes for $50 an hour—with no singing.

For the first time we are being publicly humiliated because our dollar is weak. Some ask, "Has God let us down?"

People have different answers. The most popular one is, "God didn't let us down—we let God down."

The White House keeps saying, "The dollar is exactly where we want it to be—or it wouldn't be there."

Another response is, "We are being punished because our moral values have sunk to a new low."

And, of course, you hear people saying, "It is all Alan Greenspan's fault."

If there is any solace in all this, it is that the Canadian dollar is weaker than the American one. This causes friction between our neighboring countries, but there is nothing they can do about it—except field a good hockey team.

I am sure the dollar will come back, particularly if China buys more American toys than we buy Chinese ones.

When I told a friend that France is attacking our money he said, "What else is new?"

A Vivid Inauguration

CAN YOU REMEMBER where you were when Jimmy Carter was sworn in as president of the United States?

I can, because I was there.

ABC TV, in its ultimate wisdom, had hired me to be one of its commentators at Carter's inauguration. I imagine they thought I could boost their ratings.

This is true, so don't call and ask if I made it up. I am not making it up.

My first assignment, for which I was dressed exactly like my idol, Mike Wallace, was to sit in a booth across from the White House with Harry Reasoner, and comment on the parade.

It was just the two of us and we were having a very good time. The producer kept saying, "Keep it light."

Somewhere in No Man's Land (or in this case, No Woman's Land), Barbara Walters was working the crowd. She suddenly appeared in our booth. In those days Barbara was a feisty reporter who realized the action was where she was. Barbara took over and Harry and I just sat there biting our knuckles.

But that isn't the story.

That evening I was assigned to cover one of the balls at the Sheraton Washington Hotel. It was jammed with thousands of happy revelers. I was told to stand at the end of the ballroom with a producer, in case Jimmy Carter's mother came that way.

One hour, two hours passed—no mother.

Then I realized I had to tinkle. The washroom was miles away at the other end of the ballroom. I said to the producer standing next to me, "I have to tinkle."

The producer radioed to the TV booth high up, "He has to tinkle."

A voice came down from the sky, "Tell him to stay where he is. It is not in his contract that he can tinkle. I don't want to hear about his plumbing problems."

There was agony on my face. The voice on high was saying one thing; my kidneys were saying just the opposite. Did I tell you I am on the advisory board of the National Kidney Foundation?

As luck would have it, I found an empty beer can on the floor. I also saw a heavy velvet curtain next to me. I told the producer, "I am going in."

Now all anyone could see were my black shoes. Two Secret Service agents took out their guns. My producer yelled, "Don't shoot! He is one of ours."

Lillian Carter never did show up.

Ever since then I have been putting the dots together. If ABC hadn't hired me I would never have been seated in the same booth with Barbara Walters. And if I hadn't been assigned to the ball at the Sheraton Washington (there were eight other balls that night), and if I hadn't been stationed miles away from the men's washroom, and if I hadn't had to tinkle and didn't almost get shot by the Secret Service, and if I had gotten a one-minute interview with Lillian Carter, today I would have the job that Barbara Walters has, at her salary, and I would be looked upon as another Dan Rather.

I don't think about it—except every four years. As I told Tom Brokaw in the back seat of a taxi, "I could have been a contender."

First Junk Call

....

ACCORDING TO MY CONTRACT I am permitted to write one column per year about my grandchild.

Well, here it is.

Corbin received his first junk call last week. Corbin is 2 years old, so there was great excitement in house about the call. It came at dinnertime, the most popular time for the calls to take place.

When my daughter-in-law picked up the phone, the voice on the other end of the line said, "May I speak to Corbin Buchwald concerning a 50-percent discount on our news magazine?"

His mother said, "He is right here."

She gave him the phone. He listened to the pitch with glee.

His mother said, "It is his first junk call. I am so proud. Corbin is not allowed to make or receive phone calls, but this is different."

Corbin listened and then occasionally said, "Um, ugh," a language he uses around the house all the time.

The pitchman, who rarely gets someone who does not hang up on him, kept talking.

Corbin, holding the phone, picked up his favorite automobile and pushed it under the table.

The whole time he was on the phone he kept smiling. After four minutes the pitchman decided his fish was off the hook and ended the call.

Corbin started to cry, assuming he had done something wrong.

The table gave him a rousing ovation, and he calmed down.

The conversation the rest of the evening had to do with junk calls.

My son, Corbin's father, asked, "How did they get his name?"

Mitchell Perlstein, a guest, said, "The people who give out birth information in the hospital probably sold it to them."

I said, "It is more sinister than that. Homeland Security keeps a file on every Corbin in America. There are several on the TSA 'No Fly' list."

Perlstein said, "I never heard of any terrorist named Corbin."

I replied, "That is probably his code name for 'Ali.'"

My daughter-in-law said, "I saw a show on television and it said the news magazines have the best lists of all. They guard them with their lives, and will pay a dollar for each new name."

"Don't forget charities," Carol Wheeler said. "I buy lists for my charity from anyone who will sell them."

"Is Corbin on your list?" I asked.

"I will check it out tomorrow."

My son said, "Why not put Corbin on the 'Don't Call list?'"

My daughter-in-law vetoed the idea. "If we do Corbin won't get anymore junk calls."

I asked, "How will he know?"

"Corbin is a very smart 2-year-old. He knows everything that goes on in the house."

I said, "The trouble with all this is every time the phone rings he'll answer it, and not all of the calls will be junk calls. It is your fault that you gave him the phone. Now he thinks everyone wants to speak to him."

Mitchell Perlstein said, "You're spoiling him. If he can take junk calls when he is two what has he got to look forward to when he's 3?"

My son suggested, "Junk mail? He loves the catalogues. When he's three he can open all of them."

My daughter-in-law said, "I am sure when he gets to be 3 he will have his own junk mail address."

At that moment the telephone rang and both Corbin and I made a dash for it. I won by a nose.

It is going to be a tough winter.

Making Extra Money

·······································

NOW THAT PRESIDENT BUSH is in power for four more years, I have to think of myself. I'd like some extra money.

I didn't have any good ideas until I read where Armstrong Williams, a conservative newspaper columnist and talk show host, received $240,000 from the Department of Education to publicize the president's "No Child Left Behind Act."

He was a partner in a public relations firm on the side, and that is how he got the account.

There is no doubt Williams did a good job and the Administration got its money's worth. Of course, there is always criticism when taxpayers' money is spent by the government without anyone knowing about it. Williams denied he had done anything more than any grubby talk show personality-columnist-public relations person would do under the circumstances.

Then it was discovered Williams had lost his moral compass. The media found out he received money for vocally supporting the No Child Left Behind Act. This is one of Bush's favorite programs and his people will pay $240,000 to push it through.

When I read about this, it dawned on me that I could make extra money by publicizing the president's new agenda.

First I called the Department of Education and said, "I know more children left behind than Armstrong Williams."

"We're glad to hear that," was the reply.

"Now I am willing to back it up in my column. But it will cost you."

"I don't understand."

"I want to make the same deal with you that you made with Williams. If you pay my public relations firm $240,000 dollars I will let everyone know that the No Child Left Behind Act is a slam-dunk shot."

The man on the phone said, "We have no more money in our NCLB budget for any more conflict-of-interest outsiders."

"But I have to make some government money to supplement my income."

He said, "Call the Department of Health and Human Services. They have money for columnists who are willing to write favorably about heterosexual marriage and against same-sex marriages."

"How do you know this?" I asked.

Maggie Gallagher, a syndicated columnist, is said to have been paid $21,000 form the Department of Health and Human Services to make sure everyone knows that Mr. Bush wants a constitutional amendment that, in essence, would forbid people of the same sexual persuasion to take their vows, as they can now do in Massachusetts."

I immediately called the department.

The lady was very polite. I said, "No one is more of a family man than I am. I believe in heterosexual marriage, even if it ends in divorce."

"That is fine. What do you want from us?"

"I heard the department paid Maggie Gallagher $21,000 to say the same thing."

She said, "We know where Ms. Gallagher stands on marriage vows. But we don't know where you stand."

"I will stand any where you want me to stand. I need the money."

"Submit ten columns where you have supported President Bush, and we will decide whether or not to give you the same break we gave Ms. Gallagher."

I said, "Could I have an advance?"

Social Security Blues

···································

WHEN THE COUNTRY is not worried about one thing, it is worried about another. This week's crisis is Social Security.

The President made it the cornerstone of his "State of the Union Speech," and when he tells us to worry, we better darn well pay attention.

The reaction to the speech was not all positive. For one thing, the President wasn't too sure how he wanted us to live in our old age. All he said was, if we didn't fix the system it would go bankrupt and our children and their children would have no pensions to carry them through their Golden Years.

It isn't where you stand politically that affects how you think about Social Security, it is what age bracket you are in.

Some of the reactions I heard were as follows:

Stevens said, "The President claims that Social Security will go bankrupt, but he didn't mention the national debt of 7 trillion dollars and the 427-billion-dollar deficit."

I said, "He wanted to be upbeat about the State of the Union and give a feel-good speech."

Wagshall told me, "I am 55. By the time Social Security is fixed, I will be 104 and either dead or on *The Today Show* with Willard Scott."

Not everyone who heard the speech was convinced they should worry about the children. Anderson said, "I hate my kids. I haven't seen them for two years. They blew every dollar I ever gave them, and they will blow their Social Security on booze and girls."

Of course one of the major issues has to do with Mr. Bush allowing younger people to invest in the stock market.

The Democrats are against it. Franklin told me, "The only

things young people invest in are records and rock concerts. They can't tell the difference between Enron and Google. I can just see them when the finally get to a retirement home and are unable to read the *Wall Street Journal* because the type is too small."

But the Republicans are more excited. Wall Street sees enormous future brokerage fees if people are permitted to invest in the stock market.

Oakie, a broker, said, "I will not only sell shares, but inside information to anyone who becomes my client."

It is a known fact that the TV networks do not cater to senior citizens. The reason is that people over 65 don't have any money from their Social Security to spend on what the sponsors advertise.

A seventy-nine-year-old friend told me, "I am lucky if I can get through the month on one box of corn flakes for dinner."

The fight over Social Security reform is a spectator sport and takes people's minds off of Iraq, same-sex marriage, abortions, and the Academy Awards. At dinner at tables all over the country people are discussing what to do with their parents.

Elderly people don't trust the government, and as Brinkerrhoff said, "Why should we?"

The only hope senior citizens have is that they can now get Viagra on Medicare.

Flip-Flop Diplomacy

NO ONE THOUGHT that after the election President Bush would be the one doing all the flip-flopping. In his first term he made a lot of countries mad at him when he invaded Iraq, but he didn't seem to care.

We Americans supported him (except for the anti-war traitors).

Now he is flip-flopping and on his trip to Brussels he told Europe we need each other, and the U.S. wants to be friends again.

The State Department Assistant Secretary for Flip-Flopping explained the new policy to us. "The President now loves everybody."

"Even France?" I asked.

"Yes, even France. Americans can once again eat French fried potatoes, French onion soup, go on French leave, and even French kiss."

I said, "That is certainly a flip-flop. What about Germany?"

"We don't see anything wrong with Germany anymore. You can now order sauerbraten, schnitzel, drink beer from Munich, and German kiss."

"That's nice," I said.

"We have opened an entirely new policy in our relations with, as Don Rumsfeld used to call it, the 'Old Europe.'"

"This means we don't have to boycott our friends anymore?" I asked.

"Au contraire. We have to embrace them and tell them how much we love them," he replied.

"Just when you put Americans in one mode, you ask us to change to another one."

"It can be done. If the president is willing to make up with the countries he thought did him in, everyone should do the same thing."

"Flip-Flopping is one of most important posts in the State Department.

How did you get it?" I asked.

"I was on Condoleezza Rice's National Security team. When she realized the U.S. could no longer go it alone, she told me the president asked for the most dedicated flip-flopper on her staff—a post that doesn't need congressional approval."

"And your duties?"

"I go where our leader goes and I have a briefcase full of flip-flops he can use on any of his stops."

I said, "Despite his flip-flopping, his unpopularity in Europe is still at an all time high. The man on the street, the Champs Elysee that is, doesn't believe we did the right thing by going into Iraq."

He replied, "We don't care what the man in the street thinks. Our flip-flopping is concerned with the leaders. If we can win their hearts and minds, and also buy French perfume, we will consider it a major diplomatic victory."

"They say the president has never been too interested in foreign affairs."

"That is true, but it is a plus and not a minus. Since he is not emotionally involved he can switch horses in midstream, and coming from Texas, he knows how to do it."

"Spoken like a true diplomat," I declared.

"Do you think that someday the president will flip-flop on Iran, Syria and North Korea?"

"Not at the moment, but now that the elections are over we are waiting to flip-flop on who will be Prime Minister in Iraq. If our guy doesn't get in, we will announce we always wanted the candidate who does win."

He continued, "The nice thing about a democracy is the president can flip-flop anytime he wants to, and still do great in the polls."

Harvard, Dear Harvard

AS EVERYONE KNOWS, Harvard is in crisis. It is not in as much crisis as Social Security, but it is in enough of a crisis to be on the front pages for something other than winning a Nobel Peace Prize.

The trouble started when Harvard's President, Larry Summers, delivered a speech in which he said, among other things, that women were not as successful in engineering and math as men. He also said that men would work eighty hours a week, while women had other things to do. (Read: give birth, clean, cook, and raise a family).

This and other gender and ethnic slurs enraged the faculty, and they held angry meetings where Summers was pilloried and denounced by professors for sullying Harvard's good name.

As with any crisis, there are two sides of the story. On one you have an unyielding university president who speaks out on academic issues, but also raised the school endowment by millions. And since he was a former secretary of the treasury, he has clout in Washington. The alumni and the Board of Governors backed him, and the students were split on his remarks.

On the other side were the faculty, who accused him of being abrasive and using his position to speak publicly on issues that they considered politically incorrect.

While this began as an in-house crisis, it became everybody's problem when it got into the newspapers and on TV.

The country became divided. Those who believe Harvard is the Taj Mahal of learning (students and alumni) were grief stricken that their school's name was muddied.

The campus filled up with more national reporters than the number of attendees at a Harvard-Yale football game.

President Summers brought the gender gap out of the closet.

It is sad to say not everyone cried for Harvard. Many people enjoyed its misfortune. These were not Harvard people, but those who didn't go to the university.

Harvard is considered by many to be an elite school attended by snobs, who look down on everyone, and let them know it. To say you went there is enough. It is a smug indication that you are on the top of the educational food chain. As far as Harvard is concerned, Yale, Princeton and other Ivy League institutions are no more than trade schools, where you learn how to build bookshelves.

Unlike Notre Dame, which is beloved by everyone, Harvard has never had a Knute Rockne, or a former president who asked the coach to "win one for the Gipper."

I am not one who enjoys bashing the school because of what Larry Summers said. I flunked math and science, so I can sympathize with women who are not too good at these subjects. Also, I have no problem working an 80-hour week, especially since I don't belong to a longshoreman's union.

Underneath their hubris, Harvard people are just like you and me, ready to take on the world by hook or crook or networking.

The Larry Summers remarks will blow over. Someday a woman will invent a new light bulb that will never go out. Thanks to paltry Social Security payments, everyone, men *and* women, will have to work 80 hours a week—at three different jobs.

Like so many people who never went to Harvard, the Summers flap is not my problem, but that doesn't mean we can't sit back and enjoy it.

Well Hello, Martha

Well hello, Martha
Welcome home Martha
It's so nice to have you back where you belong.
You're looking swell, Martha
You've been through hell, Martha
You're still glowin', you're still crowin'
And still coming on strong.
We hear the money tinkle
We see the profits twinkle
One of our favorite stocks from way back when…
Wow, wow, wow
Martha never go away again.

Martha Stewart paid her dues and is home (or at least serving the rest of her sentence there).

The world is a better place now that Martha once again can go about her business and tell the rest of us how to mind ours.

It goes without saying there will now be thousands, no millions, of jokes about her on the Internet, in beauty parlors, and at office water coolers, not to mention Jay Leno, David Letterman and *Saturday Night Live.*

What makes this such a great country is that when someone gets in trouble the rest of us can laugh at him or her. But the jokes have a short shelf life and soon go stale. Then we become ashamed. I have a plan for when this happens.

Every time you tell a Martha Stewart joke or hear one, you have to send a $10 check to the tsunami relief fund ($20 if you have heard the joke before).

If someone uses a Stewart joke on television he has to donate $2,500 to rebuild Sri Lanka.

The fact that someone tells a joke about Martha doesn't mean he doesn't admire her. We sleep on her sheets, bake her cupcakes, and smell her roses. When we go into a Kmart (now Sears) Martha is everywhere. We find her in the bookstores peering from magazine racks, and the Web. As a wise man said, "it's Martha's world—we just live in it."

Is Martha a better woman for being found guilty of insider trading? The Wall Street pundits are split on what she did. Fifty percent say she should never have been tried, and the other fifty percent say she was guilty, not of insider trading, but of making the paltry sum of $40,000 on the deal.

It's too late to cry over spilled milk, or Martha's cream puffs. The future is now, or as another press agent said, "Today is the beginning of the rest of Martha's life—as long as she sells more advertising pages for her *Living* magazine and has a hit television show."

No matter where you stand concerning her, you have to admit she is a household name—more famous than Janet Jackson or Betty Crocker.

The public is the jury. Will she once again become a billionaire, or will she have to live on her Social Security checks? Will she be remembered for the quilts she made in Bedford, New York, or those sewn during the last five months in Alderson, West Virginia?

Because I've devoted so much space to Martha Stewart, I am sending a $100 check for the tsunami victims in care of Bill Clinton and George Bush, Sr.

Okay, all together now, "Hello, Martha, well hello Martha, it's so nice to have you back where you belong . . ."

Smoking Guns

"THE CLASS WILL COME TO ORDER. Today we will discuss the 'Smoking Gun,' the most important subject you will learn in Law School. Who knows what a 'Smoking Gun' is? The man in the back."

"A smoking gun is a piece of evidence that is produced in a trial, most of the time as a surprise to the other side."

"Very good. Where will you find a smoking gun? The lady over there."

"The best place to find it is in e-mails that people have sent to each other because they never dreamed a third party would read them."

"Example please?"

"I am the plaintiff's lawyer in a suit against an automobile company. I want the in-house e-mails written by executives pointing out the brakes don't work, the vehicle rolls over when another car passes it, and the wheels fall off when you go down a hill. If I can prove the company knew all this I have my 'smoking gun.'"

"Good answer. So the first thing you must confiscate is a defendant's computer before they erase the messages on it. In most cases you need a judge's order. Now who knows of any other examples?"

"*Enron v. United States.* The government used the company's confidential e-mails to prove fraudulent bookkeeping, greed, conspiracy, offshore banking and natural gas that never existed."

"Professor, what if I defend Enron executives?"

"Then be sure and get your fee in advance. Now, next question. What is a perfect 'Smoking Gun' case? The gentleman in the front."

"That's easy—the state of New York against General Electric."

"What was the smoking gun?"

"The Hudson River."

"Professor, do most Smoking Guns come from computers?"

"No. Many come from whistleblowers. Let's us say an ex-employee at a drug company found out that an antidepressant caused depressions. The whistleblower would produce e-mails proving the executives insisted on doubling their advertising budget to sell the pill before the FDA made them take it off the market."

"Professor, suppose I was defending the drug company?"

"Then you would try to prove the whistleblower was a disgruntled employee, a wife beater, and someone who cheats at solitaire."

"Are smoking guns permitted in court under the Second Amendment?"

(Laughter)

"That is not as funny as it sounds. There will be lots of work for you when you get out of school defending gun manufacturers, dealers, and the National Rifle Association who, every day, are being sued by the relatives of people who were shot. The most important thing to remember today is people on a jury have seen thousands of hours of television, and are influenced by what they have seen. On every show it ends with the good-guy lawyers producing a 'smoking gun' and the bad guys going off to jail. You will never see a *Law and Order* segment with a hung jury."

A Constitutional Solution

WILLIAM SHAKESPEARE became a celebrity when he said, "Kill all the lawyers."

A serial conservative friend of mine, Sam Sampson, went one step further and said, "Let's kill all the judges."

I whistled. "Does this mean you want to pull the rug out from under the judicial system?"

"Yes. If they don't want to interpret the Constitution as we know it, then I say off with their robes."

"But if you are for Right to Life you are not supposed to kill anybody."

"There can always be exceptions."

"Judges are human like everybody else," I said.

"Not necessarily. There are human judges and non-human judges."

"How can you tell the difference?"

Sampson said, "All you have to do is read their decisions and watch their body language."

"How would you know?"

"You may not know, but our people do."

"Meaning those who believe in the Right God?"

"I am not going to name names."

"Are there some judges that you don't want to kill?" I asked.

"Yes. All the ones the president has nominated that the Democrats won't confirm because of their ideology. Their party would rather filibuster than confirm."

I said, "Senator Frist says the same thing."

"The thing we are most concerned about is the Supreme Court. Sooner or later a justice has to be replaced. And we don't want a turncoat, who, once he gets affirmed, votes in favor of *Roe v. Wade*," Sampson said.

I said, "Supreme Court justices are funny that way. Once she gets in she has a mind of her own."

Sampson said, "The only ones we can count on are Scalia and Thomas."

I agreed. "You can say what you want to about them, but they are always on the Right side."

I then said, "Here is one thing I don't understand. Why do the Right-to-Life people believe in the death penalty?"

Sampson said, "In many states it is the law. But people on death row can escape execution if they have a living will. That's a joke."

"I like it when right-wing people joke. It makes them more human."

Sampson said, "Can we get serious? The court system is in a mess and has to be reformed."

I asked, "What should we do?"

"We must file a 'Friend of the Court' brief on cases we like, and an 'Enemy of the Court' on cases we don't."

"Why are you so bitter about liberal judges that now sit on the bench?"

"In the case of federal ones, they serve for life. We can't kick the liberal ones out, even if we want to."

He said, "The Right has always been against liberal judges, and for the first time our voices are being heard on radio and television talk shows."

"Then it is nothing personal, it is political?" I asked. "Where does the Right stand on the American Civil Liberties Union?"

"We don't like them. They are always taking flag-burning cases."

"If what you want comes true, the very fabric of the court system will be changed."

"And our Constitution will be obeyed as our founding fathers had in mind. The Ten Commandments will be where they wanted them to be—on court property so everyone can read them."

Oil Tasting For Snobs

IT IS NO SECRET that the price of oil is going up. But very few people have any idea what it tastes like.

Therefore when I was invited to an oil tasting event at my Exxon gas station I accepted.

The owner had his garage set up with tables. On the tables were gallons and barrels of oil from all over the world.

"How do you decide which one to sell?" I asked.

"In this market we have to take what we can get. Here is a new barrel of Saudi Arabian that just arrived. It has a beautiful color and an aroma you won't find in other Middle Eastern countries."

He gave me a cup to taste.

I said, "It has a nutty taste, but goes down smoothly. I think it has a lot of promise." I spit it out.

"We will age it in the barrel for another year, when the price will go up."

He continued, "Here is a Kuwait Desert Red. It only can be found in the southern part of the country. I find people with SUVs prefer it over the Libyan Beaujolais, which is mixed with a cheap Algerian product."

I took a sip, then swirled it around and spit it out. "I'll take the Kuwait anytime." I then asked, "Are there some years that are better for oil than others?"

He replied, "Of course there are. I would not sell an Iraqi Bordeaux while the war is going on."

"This mean the 2003s and 2004s are hardly drinkable?"

"It is not only that. The Halliburton distributor marks up every gallon three times what it is worth."

We went over to another barrel. "This is a hard-to-get Venezuelan Burgundy. The oil workers had been on strike for two years, and this is all we could buy."

Next to it was an English Channel red.

The station owner said, "English Channel red, when mixed with Norwegian Fjord, is good for trucks and school busses."

Then he told me there was still a shortage of Alaskan crude, because for the first time the Chinese are thirstier than we are.

I said, "I hear Alaskan oil is being drilled in the tundra, and moose and polar bears are always tripping over the pipeline."

He said, "Right. Since Alaskan crude comes from the Arctic, it should always be served at room temperature."

He continued. "Over here we have several barrels of Nigerian and Equatorial blends. We carry them in case a customer asks for them for his Hyundai or Kia."

I asked, "Do you have any Russian samples for tasting?"

"They are starting to become very popular. A Russian Ivanovich is being swallowed up by European cars like the Mercedes Benz, Volvo, and BMW."

"And the Volkswagen?" I asked.

"Yes, but only if you pay in Eurodollars." Then the owner said, "That's about it. A year ago we sold a gallon of regular for $1.40. Now it is $2.40."

"Same gas?"

"Would you like a blindfold test?"

"Why not?" I said.

He put a red bandana around my eyes. I tasted five of them. As far as I was concerned, like most Americans, I couldn't tell the difference.

The News

....

HOW DO PEOPLE get their news? Let me count the ways.

In the old days I got my news primarily from newspapers, then radio, followed by television and, in the last few years, on the Internet. It is a tortuous path, but as Walter Cronkite might say today, "That is the way it is now."

Let me give you an example.

Tom DeLay. My first solid news came from a friend who claimed he heard it in a bar on K Street.

He said Congressman Tom DeLay, the Republican majority leader, took a trip to Great Britain in 2000, with a stopover at the St. Andrews golf course in Scotland. It was partially paid for by the Choctaw Indian tribe, who wanted gambling permits in Mississippi in the worst way.

It was confirmed on my car radio when I left the bar.

When I got home I saw it on CNN.

The Washington Post printed the congressman's escapade on page 1, pointing out a lobbyist for the Choctaws had helped finance the trip. An earlier story said the indictment of DeLay's close associates (charges DeLay claims were politically motivated) had Republican lawmakers worried the majority leader might be forced to step aside.

I couldn't believe DeLay, a former undertaker, could do anything wrong—certainly not play golf with Indian tribe money at St. Andrews.

But I needed more verification.

I went to my computer and typed in "www.DeLay/Indian Gambling@St.AndrewsGolf.com."

My computer came up with hundreds of Google results.

There was, "DeLay plays golf with Indian gambling money," and another one, "Rich fat cats in Texas meet with DeLay to discuss moral values," and "Oil executives count on DeLay to pass legislation giving them tax breaks."

I was disappointed I couldn't find "DeLay golf scores" either on Google or Yahoo. But I had enough information to confirm the story was for real.

The next thing I read was from the bloggers.

There was message after message for and against the congressman.

One blogger wrote, "Tom DeLay doesn't like gambling, but he has to think of who will pay for his trips abroad."

Another said, "There are few Choctaws in Houston, but I am going to get the ones who live there to vote for DeLay."

It was not only the Indians who financed DeLay's trip to Britain, but also the Christian Right, who are supposed to be against gambling and same-sex marriage.

Tommy, from Greenwich, wrote, "The Democrats are giving golf a bad name."

So, as we say in the newspaper business, the story had legs.

I filed it away because DeLay is now making news every day. It is my duty to separate the bloggers from the fair and balanced media.

We are entering a new age of news. I maintain that blogging is taken as fact—so much so that many papers pick up the blogs and print it as news.

That is why I still hang out at the K Street Bar.

The Quiet Ambassador

THE ONLY REASONS his critics don't want John Bolton to be the U.S. Ambassador to the United Nations are that he is a terrible diplomat, he dislikes the U.N., he has a short temper, and he is a bully. Outside of that he is Bush's kind of appointee.

This is what his detractors fear he will do if he gets the job.

John Bolton, in a Security Council meeting, turns to the French U.N. ambassador, who has made a speech about Iraq, and says, "Oh yeah?"

The French ambassador says, "Oh oui."

"You wouldn't say that if you didn't have diplomatic immunity."

"I can say anything I want to."

Bolton says, "Let's step outside and I will knock your teeth out."

"I don't want to step outside and fight you. I am a black belt in karate and a kick boxer, but my instructions are to solve all disputes in the U.N. diplomatically."

Bolton says, "My instructions from Washington are to do anything to win. And if any country disagrees with us we will shove the veto vote down their throat. Why don't we go down to the U.N. gym and have it out with bare knuckles?"

"Monsieur Ambassador, you are, as we say in France, a *brute*—a bully."

"And you are nothing more than a cowardly frog."

"And you are a money-grubbing flea."

John says, "If we go to the top floor I will throw you out the window."

"You don't even know where the top floor is. You said in your speech that a top floor at the U.N. building is a waste of space and so are the other floors."

Bolton says, "I am beginning to lose my temper. When I lose it I throw things at people."

"I am sure you do. Put that Oil-for-Food trophy down."

"I am going to tell Condoleezza I tried to drill some sense into your dumb head."

"And I am going to tell President Chirac never to invite your president to Versailles."

Bolton leaves the Security Council floor and he sees the Cuban delegate running down the hall and chases him. The man runs into a restroom and locks the door.

Bolton bangs on the door and yells, "Fidel, or whatever your name is, if you don't come out in three minutes we will bomb Havana."

"Why now?" the delegate asks.

"Because we know you are building biological bombs to spread germs all over Miami. And even if you are not, the president would like to bomb someplace only 90 miles away."

Two of Bolton's aides drag him back to the office.

He says, "I've really had a bad day. Bring in some of the staff so I can chew them out."

After harassing them he calls Condoleezza Rice in Washington. "Madam Secretary? I am having a bad day. Whatever country we oppose votes against us. Fifty percent of all the members hate us. And 50 percent that we give aid money to despise us."

"John, we have to do what's right for America."

"I would like to kick the Russian ambassador in the you-know-where."

"Don't do it until the president gives the word. How are you doing with the Chinese over North Korea?"

"I am not talking to the Chinese ambassador."

"Why not?"

"Because he won't apologize for parking his limousine in my reserved space."

"You've done a great job and we appreciate it."

Bolton says, "Thank you. I think I have done well, considering I have only been here two weeks."

Happy Mountain

A WISE MAN ONCE told me, "War is hell, but it is good for the economy."

He was talking about the Pentagon's announcement that it intends to close down military bases all over the country. What he really was talking about was "jobs."

Nobody wants a war, but he or she wants to manufacture the stuff that you need to fight one.

Even your most dovish congressman or senator does not want to close a military installation in his or her own back yard.

Congressman Everett F. Livid said, "You don't close bases to save money. That is not the American way. I will fight or filibuster any attempt to chop the installation at the Happy Mountain Air Force base in my district."

"But the Cold War is over."

"It could start again at any moment, and I want this country prepared to bite the bullet."

"But Rumsfeld says by closing the bases he will save taxpayers billions of dollars."

"It isn't his money, it's the taxpayers' money."

"Why don't you be honest about it? If your base is closed and 14,000 people are put out of work, it could cost you the next election."

Livid snapped, "What a terrible thing to say. We have to give our brave boys the best defense money can buy. I have been in Iraq and every soldier thanked me for what we are doing for them at home."

"Do you think the president approved of Rumsfeld's hit list?"

"I am sure he didn't know anything about it."

"How do you know?"

He was surprised and told me the only thing he is interested in is Social Security reform. I pointed out that if people could invest in the stock market, and the bases were closed, the military industrial complex bubble would burst, and people would lose their savings.

"What you were telling the president in effect is, if he allows Rumsfeld to close the base in your district, you would not vote for his Social Security reform."

"I wouldn't put it that way. Look, the economy of Happy Mountain feeds off of the base—barbers, real estate, coffee shops, and Wal-Mart. McDonald's has announced it is ready to pull out if the base is closed."

"Have you told Alan Greenspan about this?"

"All he cares about is raising the interest rate."

"How do you feel about the closings of bases in other states?"

"I don't care about them. If we are going save money I prefer the other states take the hit."

I told Congressman Livid, "This is the first time I've seen you so livid."

"How can I go home and face the people who thought I would protect them?"

"It won't be easy," I admitted. "But what Rummy says and what he does are two different things. The pressure is going to be on him."

"If the plan goes through, and the people at the base protest in the streets, it will be safer to go to Iraq than Happy Mountain. I have just begun to fight. And so has everyone in congress. Our slogan is, 'Don't Close Our Bases — Close Theirs.'"

"That's a good banner to hang on Main Street," I said.

"That, and, 'War Is Hell, but It Still Buys Your Groceries.'"

Where Were You?

HERO OR TRAITOR? That is what people are calling "Deep Throat" (a.k.a. Mark Felt).

People are choosing up sides, as they usually do, when an important news event takes place.

The ones who always believed Watergate was a nasty piece of work consider him a hero.

He put his career and his life on the line to save the country from Richard Nixon. At the time, he was the most important whistle-blower in the government.

For over thirty years no one knew who he was. Of course he is a hero to Woodward and Bernstein because he made them famous and rich and a credit to their profession.

Mr. Felt is admired in circles that believe in the Constitution and hate presidents who cover up crimes for the sake of politics.

I must admit I am one of Felt's hero worshippers.

I always suspected when Nixon said, "I am not a crook," that he was one, and when he started talking to the paintings on the White House walls, that he was going around the bend.

I believed everything Woodward and Bernstein wrote and I trusted them.

Not everyone in America believed Deep Throat was a hero. When the story of his identity broke, the television news producers yelled, "Get me anyone who was involved with Watergate and is mad at Mark Felt."

I watched a stream of people who worked for Nixon parade across the TV screen. Most of them had been in jail, so it was not surprising they would not be kind to one of the people who had put them there.

Pat Buchanan was bitter (when is he not?) and called Mr. Felt a "snake." He then charged that Felt was responsible for thousands of deaths in Vietnam because of causing anti-war demonstrations.

You figure that one out. I couldn't.

John Dean III said the information Deep Throat supplied was only 50 percent correct. He claimed there would be egg on "Throat's" face when all the facts come out.

Charles Colson said Felt was wreaking revenge on Nixon because he was not made the head of the FBI.

Gordon Liddy, who has his own radio show, had nothing good to say about Felt. He said the only reason for revealing his identity now was to make money on a book.

By the way, Felt did not leak information to the reporters. He just confirmed things they already knew.

Several of those of the "traitor" persuasion had mixed feelings about it. They, like Al Haig, didn't approve of what Felt did, but were relieved they no longer had to prove it wasn't them.

Some of the major players that Deep Throat confirmed to Woodward and Bernstein keep showing up on the TV screen.

Nixon and John Mitchell are now in that Watergate in the sky. Others, like Bob Haldeman, Jeb Magruder, and Howard Hunt are still around, but have lost faith in the FBI.

The story won't die. For years people will ask each other, "Where were you the night Deep Throat was in a garage?"

The only ones who can truthfully say are Woodward and Bernstein.

Hate in America

MILTON SAID, "Why does everyone write about how much the world hates America, and no one writes about why Americans hate each other?"

"I was thinking about it," I said. "Why do you think they do?"

"I can't blame it ALL on President Bush, but the hate factor in the country was raised to a new high when he said it was politically correct to do it."

"How so?"

"Hating fellow Americans didn't become serious until Bush decided to invade Iraq. Then both sides came out of the closet. The conservatives said war was a dandy idea, and the liberals said it was a lousy one. When it was discovered that there were no weapons of mass destruction, which was the reason for going to war, the liberals attacked the president. The conservatives called the anti-war people 'traitors.'"

"That was strong language," I told Milton.

"Adding gasoline to the fire were the 'elite' media (the *L.A. Times*, *Washington Post*, and the *New York Times*) who editorialized that we got into a lousy war and didn't know how to get out."

Milton continued, "Commentators like Bill O'Reilly and Rush Limbaugh told Americans to hate the liberals. It was a sure fire way of getting ratings."

"I hate O'Reilly and Rush Limbaugh," I said, "because they hate me."

Milton said, "But what is really tearing the country apart is God. Every group insists they know what God wants for America. People are fighting over the Pledge of Allegiance in the schools, the Ten Commandments on government property, and whether Americans came from Adam and Eve or from monkeys."

"I thought we settled that years ago," I said.

"So did most Americans, but the theories kept popping up," Milton told me. "Things really got ugly when the religious right said if you don't believe in Jesus then you are going to hell.

"Evangelicals are now going all over the country asking—no demanding—that everyone be born again. The worst example is the Air Force Academy, where the cadets are asked to pledge their lives to Jesus. No one knows what blue skies they will fly into once they graduate.

"Everything has a religious background. The Right to Life people are against stem cell research, abortions, and condoms. They are for guns, the Second Amendment, and the National Rifle Association.

"One of the major issues is same-sex marriage. The Right opposes it and the Left, who could not care less, says, 'Get off my back.'"

I said, "Isn't it now true that members of Congress really hate each other?"

"It is worse than ever. There used to be civility in both houses. They once threw buns at each other, now they throw rocks."

"I guess they can't pick a judge now without getting mad," I said. "Are all these issues political?"

"No," Milton replied. "They are personal. Americans are not born to hate—it is taught to them at an early age—and once you learn it you will never let it go."

"Tell me this. Do the French hate Americans as much as we hate each other?"

"It's a close call, but we are catching up to them. I could go on and on listing the causes as to why there is so much animosity among Americans, but it won't do anyone much good.

"All I know is, I am right and they are wrong—and I am certain they will go to hell before I do."

Bless This House

NO ONE LIKES to have his or her home taken away for no good reason. But you can't stop progress. And if the city or town wants to seize and tear down property under "eminent domain," the Supreme Court, by a 5-to-4 vote, has given them permission.

One of the first places to have been affected was Happy Valley, a community whose houses date back to the Revolutionary War.

Happy Valley overlooks the Chipchop Lake, only 40 miles from New York City.

The residents are as happy as any can be these days, considering the price of gasoline, the war, and a recent high school drug problem, which is now under control.

The day after the Supreme Court ruling, the three Happy Valley supervisors and noted developer Simon Legree, arrived at the Fenstress property. The house was built soon after the revolution, and has been lived in by members of the family ever since.

Legree took his out his digital camera and said, "It will be perfect. The shopping mall will be over there by the magnolias, the condos where those trees are now, and a business tower will be here, when we bulldoze the house."

Fenstress came out of his house and asked the group, "What's up?"

Legree said, "Nothing that concerns you. These supervisors want to make this place a decent one for everyone. If it means taking your property away, that is the way the cookie crumbles."

"You can't do that," Fenstress said. "It is my house and I have no intention of selling it."

"You apparently have never heard of 'eminent domain,'" a supervisor said. "We are not going to seize your land, we are going to *improve* it."

He continued, "Mr. Legree is one of the greatest developers on the East Coast. Whenever he sees a farmhouse he thinks 'Wal-Mart.'"

Fenstress said, "I'll sue."

The case has already been decided," Legree snorted. "The Supreme Court has ruled that you can't stop the building of a Holiday Inn just to keep your house."

"The Constitution says a man's home is his castle," Fentress said.

"Not anymore," said Legree. "A man's home is whatever the developer wants it to be."

A supervisor said, "We are not talking about land—we are talking about taxes. One Dunkin' Donuts is worth more in taxes than you will make in a lifetime."

Fenstress was furious. "How can you do this to me?" he yelled.

Another supervisor said, "We are not doing it just to you. We are doing it to everybody in the neighborhood. Legree wants protection in case he has to expand."

"Let me ask a question," Fenstress said to the supervisor. "How much money is Legree contributing to your election campaign?"

"I resent that. We don't condemn property for political reasons. That would be unethical."

Another supervisor said, "If we thought Legree would benefit financially from tearing your house down we would not rule in his favor."

Legree told Fenstress. "You are lucky your house is going to be taken and you will get a fair price for it."

Fentress replied, "But where am I going to live?"

A supervisor said, "Ask the Supreme Court."

You Can't Sue Me

I DON'T SUE EVERYBODY, but I like to know I can if I want to. This came to mind when I read that in the Senate's final days, just before it went on vacation, it passed a bill that says I cannot not sue gun manufacturers or dealers if I am the victim of a crime.

I called up Hammer, a lawyer with Hammer, Hammer, Hammer, & Thumb, and asked him for guidance on a story.

"If a company sold a pacemaker that didn't work, could I sue them?"

"Of course. No one wants to walk around with a faulty heart."

I asked, "Asbestos—as in roof shingles and ceilings—sue or not sue?"

"Sue. A jury will be on your side."

"You find a ball bearing in a can of chicken soup."

Hammer said, "It's been known to happen, and the soup company has to take the fall."

Suppose a crooked executive of a communications company defrauds billions and billions and I lose my life savings. Can I sue him?"

"Of course you can, and we would take your case. Suing people is what lawyers are for. We have one class action suit now against a chemical company that is running arsenic in the Hudson River. Launch a suit, and they will settle out of court for millions."

"What about this one? I am in an automobile crash because the brakes on my car don't work. The automobile maker never told anyone they didn't work, but there are e-mails indicating the company was aware the brakes were faulty and could lead to death."

"You can sue them for every golden parachute that the designer of the brake will get after he is fired."

I said, "I love America, because if somebody does you wrong, you can do them wrong."

"Not so fast big boy. There are things in this country that are so holy you can't sue—even if the product is responsible for putting you in the hospital or making your wife a widow."

"What is that?"

"You can't sue a manufacturer or a dealer in guns if you get shot."

"Why not?" I asked Hammer.

"The Senate passed a bill just before going on vacation that says you can't sue anyone in the gun business because it is sacred. What it means is, if for example, someone goes to a gun show and buys a weapon to commit a crime, you can't sue the maker or dealer. It is not their fault."

"Why did the Senate pass such a bill?"

"Stupid question. They were doing it to protect the Second Amendment and to support the National Rifle Association out of fear of losing money."

"How do you feel about it?" I asked

"I'm a lawyer. They are taking business away from me. At the same time, I believe that the Senate is looking out for my best interests. If we allow lawsuits against gun manufacturers the courts will fill up, and then you will have to wait a long time to sue for the things the senators say you *can* sue for, such as sex abuse in the workplace."

Therefore, when it comes to guns, their manufacturers had a great victory. The Senate's bill says you can't sue gun makers and dealers for the misuse of a firearm during the commission of a crime. If someone goes to a gun show and then uses the purchased gun to commit a crime, you can't sue the maker and dealer who did no more than provide the weapon of choice.

The senators passed this bill to protect the U.S. gun manufacturers and to keep the NRA happy.

Canceling Out O'Reilly

WHEN THE VIETNAM WAR was going on, a man stood in front of Secretary of Defense Robert McNamara's window at the Pentagon and set himself on fire to protest the war.

Mr. McNamara said it was one of the darkest moments of his life.

Last week in Crawford, Texas a "Gold Star Mother" who lost her son in Iraq, held a vigil outside George Bush's ranch to protest the Iraq war.

The press covered it and the pro-war supporters attacked Mrs. Cindy Sheehan for spoiling the president's vacation.

Leading the attacks was Bill O'Reilly, the Fox TV spinmeister, who said that the mother was being supported by the far Left who are against the war.

When I watched him on TV, Bill was mad. When he gets mad his face gets red and he demands that somebody do something about it. He wants to fire judges, impeach prosecutors, and he lets you know in no uncertain terms how he feels about the "far Left media."

The night I watched him (before Mrs. Sheehan left Crawford because her mother had a stroke) he told us that Mrs. Sheehan was to be on his show, but canceled. O'Reilly hates people who won't go on his program, and lets us know about it. He feels he is giving them an opportunity to debate with him (he doesn't let his guests talk). He behaves like the kid in school you always hated.

The more O'Reilly railed against Mrs. Sheehan, the more supporters he made for her. Many who came to Crawford planted white crosses on the highway.

O'Reilly said she was a puppet of ideologues who were using her to embarrass President Bush.

He went on to say that Mrs. Sheehan flip-flopped on President Bush's role in the war. Bill hates someone who flip-flops, especially when he thinks they should flip and not flop.

It isn't easy to trash a mother who lost her son in Iraq, but

O'Reilly has managed to do it. He has tied Mrs. Sheehan up with Michael Moore, MoveOn, and Maureen Dowd.

O'Reilly said he only deals in facts and told us Cindy's husband was getting a divorce from her, which says more about what kind of woman she really is.

What started out as a vigil in Crawford became an anti-war protest. Reporters from all over the world showed up. Mrs. Sheehan appeared on every television show (why didn't she appear on Bill O'Reilly's?).

President Bush was shown trying to have a vacation, while the protestors stood outside the ranch holding up signs against the war.

It was Viet Nam déjà vu all over again.

The President, Donald Rumsfeld, and Condoleeza Rice were assuring us things are getting better in Iraq if we "just stay the course." People who refused to stay the course were not loyal Americans. Holding vigils in Crawford could be compared to immolation in front of the Pentagon.

The questions flew all over the lot. "Why doesn't Cindy go home and leave the President alone? He is the Commander-in-Chief, and like Lyndon Johnson, he knows how to fight a war."

The O'Reilly Factor went by so fast I hated for the hour to be over.

I didn't know at the end whether Bill was mad at Cindy for being used by the Left or because she never went on his show.

Darwin Go Home

WHAT DID I DO last summer? Part of the time I sat on the beach discussing Darwin versus creationism. Those who believed in Darwin sat on one side of the sand and used sun tan oil, because scientists say you don't want to burn your skin.

On the other side were the creationists, who maintained they didn't need oil because God would protect them.

One religious bather said, "Darwin didn't know what he was talking about. I did not come from a monkey—or even a horse."

A Darwin supporter said, "Conventional wisdom says the creationist belief is just a theory, while Darwinism is a science."

"If creationism is just a theory in the Bible," a born-again Christian said, "Why does President Bush want it taught in the schools?"

"It's good for him politically, and shows he believes in God," I said. "I can believe in Darwin and God, but I don't believe creationism should be taught as science in public schools. Besides, I thought the question was resolved years and years ago."

There was stirring from the right. "Anyone who says that doesn't believe in God."

"I am not an atheist. I go to church every Sunday, but that doesn't mean I have to buy the Adam and Eve story. I still want to know who wrote it."

Things were getting more heated. The Darwin supporters started to kick sand at the creationists.

I tried to get the discussion back on track. "Intelligent Designers have no proof as to how life began, but we still have to respect their beliefs."

A Darwin spokesman said, "I don't say there is no God. All I am saying is there is no proof there is one."

An evangelical retorted, "Proof is in the eye of the beholder. Anyone who doesn't believe in Intelligent Design is a pagan."

"And who is the father of Intelligent Design?"

"The people who wrote the Bible. They knew God's words had to be passed on. Everything was just fine until Darwin took a trip around the world and said we descended from animals."

"Why do people hold such a grudge against Darwin? He brought order to the human race. The Intelligent Designers have been fighting with each other for thousands of years," a scientist said. "Even today they are arguing about God."

"Yes, but you need scientists to provide the weapons used against people who don't believe in your theory. You can't have strong beliefs without guns to back them up."

A creationist who was building a sand castle said, "How do we know Australopithecus wasn't a hoax?"

The Darwin man retorted, "How do we know God is not a hoax?"

I said, "This is getting rough. It is tearing the people apart. Creationists live by moral standards and unquestionable beliefs. Evolutionists believe nothing unless they see it for themselves. I believe the two shouldn't be in the same ball park—or on the same beach."

"What do you suggest?"

"Let's have a volley ball game. The creationists against the evolutionists."

A scientist said, "I'll play only if the playing field is level."

An Intelligent Designer replied, "God always makes the playing field level. That is why we love him."

Katrina

...

SOMETIMES AN EVENT is so staggering it is impossible to absorb. And so it is with Hurricane Katrina.

We are all involved, and as I watched my television screen, my mind kept jumping around and was unable to stay on any one part of the tragedy for long.

The immediate messenger was television. The reporters stood in front of destroyed houses and debris and told us what they saw over and over again.

First came floods, and then came the rescues. Then, because it was good television, came the pictures of the looters.

The National Guard arrived on the scene, but as the waters receded, the blame-sayers went into action.

Why didn't the U.S. Army Corps of Engineers predict what would happen in a Category 5 hurricane? How come the state did not communicate with the federal government, and how come it was so slow in going into action? And how come no one knew the Super Dome would leak?

Why did the president take so long to tell us the recovery would take such a long time? What will it do to the nation's budget? How will Katrina affect the price of gasoline?

Questions . . . nothing but questions.

As I looked at all the destroyed homes I thought, "People lived in those houses. They had families and all their worldly possessions were washed out to sea."

Was Katrina an "act of God" as some insurance companies may claim, or did it have anything to do with global warming?

It is hard to absorb the numbers. How many dead, how many refugees, how many homeless?

So the hurricane becomes personal. You know people in New Orleans; you know people who knew people.

I know a lovely lady named Ella Brennan. She owned one of the finest restaurants in New Orleans, Commander's Palace. Whenever I went to New Orleans I made the restaurant my first stop. Ella and I talked politics. We both thought alike and had many friends in common. It was the conversation as much as the food that attracted me.

At this moment I don't know where Ella is, but I care very much. Somebody else's tragedy is really yours when you know the people involved. No matter how far we are removed from the Mississippi, we are affected.

I feel stupid writing about the effects of Katrina from so far away. But I would feel stupid not writing about it.

We will hear about Katrina for weeks, possibly months, and then it will fade away, except for those who were there. They will never get it out of their minds.

We will have congressional hearings, commissions appointed by the Justice Department, and, politics being politics, the disaster will become a big issue in the next election.

The jury has yet to be called to decide who was right and who was wrong. Until then all we can say is, "No man is an island. Ask not for whom Katrina blows, she blows for thee."

Once Upon a Time in New Orleans

ONCE UPON A TIME in New Orleans, as everybody remembers it, is no more. This much we know now. The bottom line is no longer the bottom line. Everything about the American Dream has been washed into the sea.

People on the Gulf have no jobs, no money, no clothing, and have lost all their possessions.

How do we know this? We saw it on television and we read about it in the newspapers.

That is where they are now in America. The people in Washington will give them money if they have none, or say they will. But you certainly can't start your life all over again on a government handout.

We now know the poor people did not have much money to start with. But even the middle class was wiped out by the hurricane.

They are now living in sports centers, trailers, or with relatives, and are on the dole. It is not a pretty picture because now they have lost their center and many are experiencing post-hurricane trauma.

Since they lost everything they had no choice but to lash out in anger. People are playing the "blame game."

It is the only game they have left to play.

As everyone who has a microphone will tell you, there is enough blame to go around for everybody. The obvious people to blame are the mayor, the governor, the Washington bureaucrats, the Army Corps of Engineers, and FEMA.

Blaming them will not put money in anyone's pocket. We know this now.

When you lose an entire city people argue whether they should rebuild it or not. The experts as well as the talking heads on TV have strong opinions, though most of them have never been in a hurricane

The president remembers when he had good times in New Orleans in his youth. He told reporters this when he flew over the city in Air Force One.

The most tired words we hear are "below sea level." Everyone knew New Orleans was below sea level, and now everyone knows the dikes would not hold when a Hurricane came along.

It is self-evident now. Under these conditions we all know everything NOW about things we didn't care to know before.

The country is full of experts sitting in their living rooms in front of their TV sets giving Monday morning quarterback opinions.

People have been very generous, either because these are fellow Americans who are suffering, or out of guilt for the victims they ignored for so many years.

The question now is, what happens the next time?

Will Homeland Security protect us? Will someone get us out of town? Will the National Guard rescue us in time? Will the director of FEMA, who was relieved of authority in New Orleans, receive the country's Medal of Honor?

These are questions we have no answers for, except from the president—and if you don't believe him you are not a patriot.

So no matter what happened, people have to face up to what they know now.

We never knew it would be this bad. No one ever imagined it.

The bottom line can now only be reached in the muddy waters of New Orleans by boat.

I'll Drink to FEMA

ROTHMAN AND I WERE drinking margaritas, just like Michael D. Brown after he was dumped as the head of FEMA.

I said, "I am frightened that I will never be evacuated out of Washington if the balloon goes up."

"Not to worry. FEMA has a plan."

"What is it?" I wanted to know.

Rothman took out a pamphlet. He showed it to me.

I read from it, "'The most important thing is not to panic and have a full tank of gas.'"

"Tell me Rothman, why should I not panic?"

He said, "Because FEMA is there to help you. That's their job. When the balloon goes up you call this private toll free number, 800-XYZ-FEMA, and leave a telephone number where you can be reached. If you don't hear from them in three days, it means they are very busy, and you are on your own. It's all in the pamphlet."

I said, "I need another margarita." I made one for myself and one for Rothman.

I raised my glass, "Here's to FEMA, which is part of Homeland Security and blessed by the Bush administration."

Rothman said, "I'll drink to that. Let's study a map and see what is the best way to get out of town."

We studied an AAA road map. "My suggestion is that we go out to the beltway after crossing Key Bridge and getting on the George Washington Parkway," Rothman said.

"Have you ever tried to get to the Beltway during rush hour?" I asked.

Rothman replied, "We will leave at midnight."

"But if we leave at midnight and their sirens go off, everyone else will leave at midnight, and the cars will be bumper to bumper. It will take us six hours to get out of town."

"Then we will go by bus. FEMA will supply people with busses. It is part of their plan."

"How will the busses get out of town if the cars can't?"

"They will have National Guardsmen on each one, and if you don't have the correct fare they have orders to shoot you."

I said, "Let's have another margarita."

Rothman agreed, "Things look so much better when you've had several margaritas."

We drank them down.

I asked, "Where do we go?"

Rothman studied the map. "West Virginia?"

"I have never been to West Virginia. Will they give us shelter?"

"FEMA will say they have to. If the people there refuse, they will set up tent cities."

I said, "FEMA is prepared for every situation. That is why they always get such a good press. What do we do for money?"

"The government will declare us poor, and will give us money slated for the Defense Department or the CIA."

"I don't want to be classified as poor," I said.

"Nobody wants to be poor. The media won't leave you alone," Rothman said. "They are always looking for poor people for the evening news."

I said, "We're dealing with a hypothetical. That's why we're getting drunk."

Rothman poured himself another drink. He slurred, "FEMA makes me proud to be a taxpayer."

"Let's toast Bush's disapproval ratings."

Rothman said, "I'll drink to that."

A Leak in the Basement

IT WAS THE LEAK that shook the world—and worse still—the *New York Times.*

The first time it showed up was when Robert Novak, known as "Hurricane Darkness," printed the name of a CIA agent who was the wife of American Ambassador Joseph Wilson, who wrote an op-ed piece in the *New York Times* that Saddam Hussein was not buying uranium from Niger to make an atomic bomb and did not have weapons of mass destruction, which was the president's excuse for going into Iraq, and which was supposed to be a piece of cake, which turned into a quagmire, causing the death and wounding of thousands of American soldiers and Marines, not to mention Iraqi citizens, and created an army of insurgents who are still there killing Iraqi soldiers because they are not ready to defend themselves without coalition forces.

Once the leak was sprung, it became a broken levee. The public demanded to find out who leaked it, and the Justice Department, under pressure, appointed a special prosecutor to investigate whether any laws were broken and how far up in government the leaker went.

It turns out the name was mentioned to six reporters, but only Novak used it, and so far, no one knows what he revealed to the special prosecutor, except he is not in contempt, as is Judy Miller, of the *New York Times,* who refused to reveal her sources and chose to go to jail instead, a noble act that recently became questionable, in part because her confidential source agreed to give her a waiver so she could get out of jail.

But she refused and stayed for 85 days.

The *New York Times* originally described her as "Joan of Arc," but after she was released they started having some misgivings because her version as to what happened conflicted in many ways with those of the *Times* reporters who were covering the story.

By this time the leakers' names were bandied about, and lo and behold, the leak came from the White House and the names I. Lewis Libby, Karl Rove, and Vice President Cheney kept popping up, and try as much as they could, they couldn't find a plumber before all the damage was done.

This is not the first time the White House has leaked, but it is the first time they got caught at it, and possibly lied to the grand jury about facts.

The whole purpose of the leak was to discredit Ambassador Wilson's reputation and destroy his story because it contradicted the White House story about weapons of mass destruction as an excuse for invading Iraq, which they believed would bring democracy to the Middle East, in spite of anti-Bush people, who would love to see Republicans lose the election in 2006 because most of the American people have recently decided that going into Baghdad was a bad idea, and made us villains all over the world.

It is not for us to decide whether a leak to a reporter can bring down the White House, at least not until the special prosecutor hands in his report.

Torture Airlines

EVERY TIME I SEE a high government official on television, he or she says, "We don't torture people."

It is a mantra and is said every day when someone in the Bush administration speaks to the press.

The phrase got new life when it was revealed by the media that the CIA was flying prisoners to countries in Asia and East Europe.

The cynics have dubbed it, "Torture Airlines."

At first the CIA denied the flights existed. But when the unmarked planes kept landing at airports around the globe, they admitted they had the planes, but denied the aircraft had anything to do with torture.

A CIA airline spokesperson said, "There is no such thing as torture in our flight book."

I said, "How can you say that when you make the prisoners sit in the middle seat with no leg room? Don't you consider that torture?"

He said, "There is nothing in the Geneva Convention that says we are not permitted to have a prisoner of war fly coach."

"It has been reported that you only give them pretzels on the flights."

"We are not going to give them a full meal, especially on our short flights to Poland and Bulgaria."

"Do you show movies on your flights?" I asked him.

"No feature films. But we will let the passengers watch Vice President Cheney making a speech to the American Legion. It may not be enough to break the POWs down, but at least it will soften them up.

He continued, "Torture Airlines plays by the rules. For example, you can't get out of your seat at takeoff or landing. If a POW has a laptop computer, he can't turn it on until we are 10,000 feet in the air."

"Has it become more expensive for you to fly since the price of fuel has gone up?"

He replied, "Our passengers travel light. They are only allowed to carry one bag on the plane, and no scissors or prayer beads. This keeps the weight down, and then we have room for 10 more terrorists who could spill the beans."

I asked, "What about frequent flyer miles for your passengers?"

He said, "We haven't gotten into that yet."

I said, "Frankly I don't understand the purpose of your airline. You say you don't torture anyone, and yet . . ."

"Who said we didn't torture anyone?"

"Condoleezza Rice, for one. She says Americans don't do that sort of thing."

He replied, "She is a nice lady, but no Secretary of State knows what the CIA is up to. She has to fly around the world assuring everyone the only reason we fly al Qaeda members to foreign lands is because we don't have any room to lock them up at home."

"Still," I said, "some people believe you deliver them to places like Egypt and Pakistan because it is easier to torture people there without the bleeding hearts finding out about it."

"We deny it. We fly people to places they have never been to before. For example our passengers have never seen the Pyramids or traveled up the Nile. 'Torture Airlines' goes to places even Delta doesn't."

I asked, "If you are not a suspected terrorist or an al Qaeda big shot can you still get a seat on the plane?"

He said, "No, we are completely sold out for a year. But if you could be a suicide bomber we will put you on the waiting list."

Let's Pretend

·················

LET'S SAY YOU are rich. Not just rich, but filthy rich. Then let's pretend what it will cost you.

You started with nothing, but then made your money investing other people's money for them.

How did you get these clients? You promised them you would double their money for them. People who have money always like to make more.

The market is at its height, and you invest their money in stocks that have to do with the computer business.

Word is out that you can make a killing for them, and the rich folks come to your door begging for you to take them on.

Before you know it, you are investing six hundred million dollars for people all over the country.

It makes you feel good and it makes them feel good.

You buy yourself homes in Florida, Paris, and a duplex penthouse on Park Avenue. You own a yacht, and you have paintings by Chagall, Picasso, Modigliani, Renoir, and Jackson Pollock on the walls.

A private plane is always at your disposal.

There is only one thing wrong. You get no respect. You are a nobody, and you want to be a somebody.

A friend who is a somebody says, "You have to become a philanthropist. The only way to get into the newspapers is to pledge money to America's cultural and educational institutions. I will take you under my wing."

You thank him gratefully and tell him, "When I become somebody I will never forget you."

He says, "To start with, pledge fifty million dollars to the

Museum of Modern Art and another fifty big ones to Harvard. Do you like opera?"

You answer, "I love opera."

"Then announce you are going to give seventy million to the Met.

"Don't stop there," your friend tells you. "M.I.T. can always use money. Give to the ballet, and also to a fund to save Venice. Once the word is out that you are an easy mark, everyone in the arts will come to you."

Now remember, you are very, very rich, and your investments are doing very, very well.

You start to notice a difference in the way people treat you. Headwaiters always have a table for you. You get into all the gossip columns, and your picture appears in the newspaper every time you go to a party.

You know you are a somebody when they ask you to put your hands in cement on the sidewalk in front of Lincoln Center.

All your friends are somebodies. You no longer have to circulate with nobodies.

So you are a very rich and contented person. Life is good, and you have fulfilled the American dream and more.

Then all hell breaks loose. The stock market where you invested everybody else's money goes down the drain.

Once you made millions—now you lose millions. The only problem is that you, as the Good Samaritan, have pledged money to all these institutions, and they would love to collect it before you go bankrupt.

Now here comes the bad news. Instead of investing all your clients' money in the market, you used it to keep up your life style.

One lady discovers her money was not invested in the market as you promised. She calls you a crook.

The Attorney General of New York State has a thing about your stealing other people's money. He announces he is going to make an example of you.

If we follow this scenario to its end, you go to jail—and still owe Harvard fifty million dollars.

The Truth About Global Warming

PRESIDENT BUSH IS COVERING all his bases. He is traveling around the United States defending his policies. The White House is scripting his appearances, and of course they depend on press coverage.

Bush's handlers points out to the president that he had not said anything about global warming, and it was becoming a sore point with the public.

One advisor says, "Let's set up a news conference and advertise the fact that the president will talk about the question of global warming."

The president agrees that it is a good idea and asks, "Where should we hold the conference?"

Another advisor answers, "What do you think about holding a fundraiser on the Arctic Ocean?"

Someone else says, "What about on the *Titanic*?"

"And we'll have a big banner saying, 'MISSION ACCOMPLISHED.'"

The president says, "I like it. What do I say about my stand on global warming?"

"You can say that the press only writes about the bad things, like the earth getting warmer and polar ice caps melting. You will announce that your environmental advisor, who formerly worked for the Petroleum Institute, said that scientists don't know what they're talking about."

Bush says, "I have never trusted scientists. They just stick with the numbers, and all they want to do is hurt us politically."

"Then, Mr. President, you will assure the country that the *Titanic* will never hit an iceberg as long as you're president. And even if it does, you will stay the course."

The president nods his head. "Can I talk about greenhouse gases that are melting the ice at both poles?"

"We think it's a good idea to say that although the emissions may be responsible for the melting, American corporations are dependent on carbon dioxide to keep their factories going. You should also say warm weather will cut down on the use of heating oil."

The president says, "This would be a good place to attack the environmentalists."

An advisor says, "If any of the scientists try to make us look silly on global warming we'll censor their reports and forbid them to attack our position."

The president asks, "Can I promise we can bring the boys home by Christmas?"

"Good idea."

An aide says, "Mr. President, your second term is only the tip of the iceberg, and you will do whatever is necessary, even though it hurts you in the polls."

Another advisor adds, "The temperature changes can't but help your popularity. You'll go down in history as the American president that warmed the world."

An environmental advisor says, "We will announce that we believe in a pre-emptive strike against floods, droughts, heat waves and hurricanes—because you think it's the right thing to do."

An advisor says, "The country will remember that you were the captain of the *Titanic*, and if it weren't for you, the ship would have struck an iceberg."

"Sir, this global warming news conference on the *Titanic* will be remembered in a league with the Gettysburg address."

"Mr. President, this will be a great photo-op."

The president asks, "Who will we put on the deck of the *Titanic* to cheer me on?

"Conservatives, anti-environmentalists, polar bears, seals, and penguins."

The Nine Trillion Dollar Heist

I TOLD KNUDSON the other day that the national deficit is now nine trillion dollars.

He said, "And what's the bad news?"

I said, "It's not as terrible as it sounds because it's only $31,500 dollars for each man, woman, and child in the United States."

Knudson said, "Well I don't have $31,500."

I said, "Well if you can't find it, you're going to have to get your kid to pay it."

"My kid would probably spend it on CDs and pot."

I answered, "Well that's not going to help us fiscally. If we're going to make our kids pay our debt, they have to get very serious.

I know they have no respect for the Boomer Generation, but we can't carry around a nine-trillion-dollar debt on our backs.

Knudson suggested, "I could hold up a bank, because that's where the money is."

I replied, "That money has already been spoken for."

Knudson asked, "How are you going to come up with the money?"

I said, "I'm lucky because I have three children and five grand-children. They promised if I couldn't pay it they would."

Knudson asked, "How can you be sure?"

I said, "My children and grandchildren have never lied to me. Also, by the time they grow up, nine trillion dollars won't be much money. It will hardly pay the salary of a good baseball player."

Knudson suggested, "Maybe we can make it an accounting problem. Every corporation seems to be cheating on their taxes. So we could just get accountants to cook the books."

"No, Knudson." I said. "You don't cheat on taxes. If we did the rest of the world would lose respect for us. This country was built on the idea of, 'No taxation without representation.' That's not true anymore because of the lobbyists."

"What would happen if every man woman and child refused to pay the nine trillion dollars?"

I said, "Perish the thought. I don't want to see little kids running around the parks refusing to contribute to reducing the deficit. We have a slogan, 'Let no taxpayer be left behind.'"

Knudson asked, "Does the deficit have anything to do with the government?"

"Heavens, no. The government is very frugal, and spends money only for things that are absolutely necessary, including war."

Knudson said, "I don't want to be pro-Bush or anti-Bush. But at the same time I don't want to owe him money."

"Why not?"

"Because I know he has a plan to pay off the nine trillion before he leaves office."

"I'm just warning you," I said. "If you don't come up with the $31,500, and if your kid doesn't, and your grandchild doesn't, the IRS will take your house away from you."

Knudson said, "Can we change the subject? I hate to talk about taxes while we're eating dinner."

I said, "I probably wouldn't bring it up if April 15th wasn't just around the corner."

Knudson said, "Well, I'll tell you this, paying taxes makes sick to my stomach."

"There are only two things that mean anything, Knudson—death and taxes. You can do something about death, but you can't do anything about taxes."

Good News

HOW DO YOU GET your news in a hospice? Just like everybody else. Some days are good days, and some are bad. Last week was full of good news.

Tom DeLay announced he wasn't going to run for Congress. In one story he said he was doing God's will. Another said he could be in trouble for raising money by doing favors.

I was not joyous when I heard the news. DeLay is one of the

few targets in Congress who is known by everyone. When I mention his name I don't even have to say, "The Hammer." I don't know whether people enjoy reading about him because he was once an exterminator, or because as the leader of the House he took favors from Jack Abramoff.

What will the media do without Tom DeLay? We'll find somebody almost as good, although we will have to wait for the next election.

The next story that the country enjoyed had to do with the president giving Dick Cheney a leak, which he passed on to I. Lewis Libby. The attorney general said the president had a right to leak secret stuff to the public if it's in our interest. I agreed because Bush is my president and I trust someone who is not afraid to leak top-secret information.

The fall guy is Libby, the vice president's aide, who passed on the information to newspaper people that former ambassador Joe Wilson's wife worked for the CIA. No one knows how the president broke the story to Cheney. I think he said, "Dick, I'm going to tell you a CIA secret. Don't tell anybody except Bob Novak, Judy Miller, or anybody else who likes to print CIA secrets."

Since Libby has not been tried yet, the story has legs and will be on the front page at least until next week.

The third good story of the week came from, of all places, the *New York Post*. The newspaper has a "Page Six" feature that prints all the gossip that's fit and not fit to print. One of the Page Six reporters was caught blackmailing a billionaire. He promised not to write anything bad about the victim if he paid $100,000 plus $10,000 a month. Ron Burkle, an investor in supermarkets and all sorts of businesses, told the FBI, and they conducted a sting operation, with photographs, tapes, and other evidence against the blackmailer.

What made it such a good story is that the *New York Times* and the *Daily News* both printed it on their front pages. This was payback time against Rupert Murdoch, who owns the *New York Post*, and, people say, Page Six was his favorite feature. What makes it an even stranger story is that the *New York Post* didn't print anything about it at all.

In any case, I liked the story because it had nothing to do with leaks from the White House.

My favorite story of the week was when an ancient scroll, the Gospel of Judas, was discovered. In the text it turns out that Judas was a good guy and when he blew the whistle on Jesus, it was Jesus' idea.

It changed a lot of people's thinking about Judas' role at the Last Supper. It now also affects people's Passover plans.

A Call from Big Brother

THE REASON AMERICANS feel safe is because the government has all sorts of ways of watching them. The feds can do it from the air, from the ground, and by mail. I feel safer if I know that somebody is eavesdropping on me.

I understand, based on information I have read, that this is how it works. The National Security Agency taps into your phone records and decides if your call is dangerous. For example, if their data bank indicates your mother calls you more than once a week, it will cross-reference the calls with how many times you called her.

Then, based on that, they can alert the FBI as to where your mother lives and her Social Security number.

The FBI may call on your mother's neighbors to find out what they know about her and how many times a week she calls them.

In case for some reason surveilling your phone calls is not sufficient, the Pentagon has its own system. They track down anybody with a foreign accent and then share this information with the CIA.

The CIA has experts in different languages who are able to trace cell phone calls anywhere in the world.

For example, suppose someone in San Diego calls his brother in Mexico and says he's sending him money so that the brother can sneak over the border into the United States.

This is a problem for the Immigration Service, which has its own data bank that is plugged into the Western Union money order department.

President Bush has assured the country that everyone's privacy is guaranteed. This even includes collect calls he makes to Putin.

But this does not mean the government isn't tapping into newspaper offices to find out who the journalists are talking to.

At this point the Justice Department gets a court order to find out who the journalist has been accepting leaks from.

Once they get the order, they can also search the homes of anyone who works for the telephone company.

A guarantee of privacy is something that all the law enforcement organizations assure the American people they will receive.

Of course, if you're a terrorist, you are not entitled to privacy—unless you are an American citizen.

Here is what to look for to find out if the government is tracking your telephone calls. If your telephone bill is much larger than you think it should be, somebody is charging calls that you haven't made.

You cannot complain to the NSA if your children have cell phones.

The easiest way for someone to spy on you is through satellites. A satellite passes over your house every few minutes.

Tracking government officials who are using their phones for personal business is harder to do.

As an American, I sleep better knowing that there are 16 intelligence agencies protecting me. If one fails, there are 15 more to pick up the ball.

The majority of American people, when polled, say they don't mind the government listening in on them, and they are known as "patriots."

Then there are those who never call their mothers. Their mothers call them ungrateful.

About the Author

ART BUCHWALD has written thirty-four books, including two children's books and two novels. His most recent novel is *Stella in Heaven* (Putnam, 2000) and his most recent collection is *We'll Laugh Again* (Putnam, 2002). He was the recipient of the Pulitzer Prize for "Outstanding Commentary" in 1982, and in 1986 was elected to the American Academy of Arts and Letters. Mr. Buchwald is a workaholic and has no hobbies.

Also by Art Buchwald